# BEDFORD
## and the
# BRITISH CHEVROLET

ISBN 1 898432 06 6

In course of preparation – Bedford Volume Two – 1950-1986

For details of other transport titles available from Venture Publications Ltd please send a stamped addressed envelope to VPL 128 Pikes Lane, Glossop, SK13 8EH

**Front Cover Illustration**

Bedford's all-time classic bus without doubt was the OB. Many thousand were produced and could be seen in service with operators large and small throughout the British Isles and abroad. Hants & Dorset Motor Services operated examples and KEL 679, superbly restored was photographed leaving Toddington after a rally in September 1994. It carries the popular Duple bodywork which will always be associated with the OB model.

*Photo J. A. Senior*

Produced for the Publishers
**Venture Publications, Glossop, Derbyshire,**
by Mopok Graphics, Glossop SK13 8EH
using computerised origination

# BEDFORD
## and the
# BRITISH CHEVROLET

by

## Stuart Fergus Broatch

### Series Editor and Designer

## Alan Townsin

Below: Many restored vehicles seen at rallies have had interesting lives and this 1932 WLG model is no exception. The chassis originally carried a horse box body built by Vincents of Reading but by the time it was purchased for restoration the vehicle had degenerated to the status of a pig shed. After full restoration it was entered in the Brighton Rally, immaculate as seen here, by Daniel Owens.

Facing page: This 1935-built WTB with 20-seat coach bodywork by Duple was photographed at Brighton in 1969. It had been supplied new to Garner's in Ealing, London, but was requisitioned by the MoS during the war. It later had two owners in Devon before being purchased by E. J. Baker of Aldershot in January 1965 and subsequently restored to its original livery.

# CONTENTS

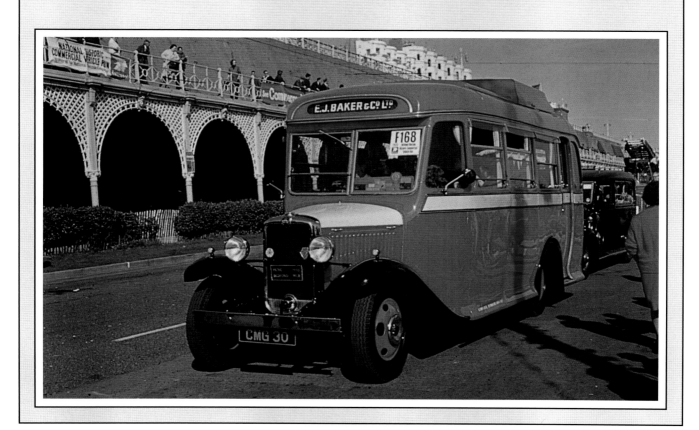

# INTRODUCTION

Bedford's WT model – the first true Bedford – appeared in June 1934 following the announcement of the model some seven months previously. Our story begins much earlier, however, since the various strands which came together in Luton when that vehicle rolled off the production line stretched back to 1857 in London and to the United States of America three years later.

Alexander Wilson founded a company called the Vauxhall Ironworks at Vauxhall, London, in 1857. After a busy but not very profitable 39 years Wilson left, following the appointment of a receiver. The reconstructed company announced the completion of its first motor car in 1903, moved to new premises in Luton in 1905, and then changed its name to Vauxhall Motors in 1907. In 1925 Vauxhall Motors was bought by the giant American company General Motors.

General Motors had also had a chequered history. Its founder, WC Durrant, was born in 1860. By 1910 General Motors was in financial difficulties and the following year Durrant was forced to relinquish his position as President. He bought a garage in Detroit and gave financial backing to one Louis Chevrolet. The first Chevrolet cars proved to be unprofitable and Durrant started the Little Motor Company with managerial and technical help from ex-Buick staff. Realising the limitations of the name Little (from the car's designer) Durrant changed it to Chevrolet (the company he had acquired through his backing of Louis Chevrolet). Durrant's Chevrolets proved successful and his investment grew such that through it he was able to regain control of GM. In 1920 – two years after GM sold its first commercial vehicle in the UK – Durrant stepped down for the last time.

From November 1925 General Motors owned Vauxhall Motors, based in Luton, Bedfordshire, in addition to assembling and selling Chevrolet commercials in Hendon. Between 1929 and 1931 UK Chevrolet production was transferred to Luton, with the first British-built Chevrolet-Bedford appearing in 1930. The first Bedford PSV left the factory in August 1931 and, as already recorded, the WT model was announced in November 1933.

Bedford was to become hugely successful but by 1986 it had become a victim of changing circumstances and was sold to AWD, being subsequently sold to Marshalls of Cambridge. This first volume takes the story to the mid-'fifties, however, a time when the world seemed to be at Bedford's feet. Many readers will remember that period with great affection and the illustrations throughout this volume will doubtless stir many memories!

# ACKNOWLEDGEMENTS

Many people have helped stimulate my interest in Bedford vehicles over the years – they have provided an insight into things seen and unseen. I would particularly like to thank the following for their assistance:

Geoffrey King, son of the late Chief Engineer C.E. King of Vauxhall Motors for technical information.
John Alden, ex-Chief Engineer, Vauxhall Motors.
Mike Bundy and Steve Muspratt, Anna Valley Motors, Salisbury, Wiltshire.
Miriam Carroll and Bob McPhee, Vauxhall Motors.
Paul Crowther, Director of Operations, Brighton Borough Council.
Charlie Hardy, Engineering Inspector (PSV), who sadly died before this book was completed.
Mr Heath, Brighton Borough Council for help with the JJL.
Rita King, CEK's daughter-in-law.
Bill Ladbrook, ex-Managing Director, David Brown Tractors Ltd.
Des Reid, Des's Coaches, my original school bus driver.
C. Rowland, Rambler Coaches, St. Leonards on Sea, Sussex, for help with the JJL and Cummins conversion.
Christopher Saleman and Steve Winbush, CVRTC.
Alan Townsin, who gave much assistance and helped bring everything   together for publication.
David Waterman, Yates in the South, Salisbury, Wiltshire.
Dilys and Pauline, for their general help and encouragement.

A special thank you is due to Vauxhall Motors and the Commercial Vehicle and Road Transport Club.

I would like to make it clear that the responsibility for any errors or omissions is mine, though I suspect my colleague Alan Townsin might agree to be involved in this responsibility!

A superbly restored Bedford MLD, dating from 1939, and kept in splendid condition by the Jellis family in Buckinghamshire. Reg Jellis is a long-standing Bedford enthusiast and his enthusiasm and willingness to help and advise have assisted others in recreating similarly magnificent examples of the marque.

# 1 A TRANSLANTIC MARRIAGE

Originally there was Vauxhall, founded in 1857 by Alexander Wilson. Fifty-one years later, in 1908, General Motors was formed in the United States by William Durant and in 1911 the first Chevrolet motor car was produced under his backing in Detroit. Both General Motors and Vauxhall had faced financial collapse before Bedford came into being. It was the success of Chevrolet in the 1920s, principally in America but also, as nowadays apt to be almost forgotten, as a large-scale commercial vehicle maker in Britain, that paved the way for the introduction of the Bedford marque in 1931.

By late 1925, General Motors was not only growing fast, with Chevrolet as its largest subsidiary, but had strengthened its position in Britain by taking over Vauxhall in the November of that year. General Motors, Chevrolet and Vauxhall had very different origins but each is sufficiently interesting to warrant a closer look.

## GENERAL MOTORS – the early years

W. C. Durant, born in 1860 in Boston, gained a reputation as an entrepreneur and wheeler dealer. He bought the then ailing Buick company in November 1904 and already owned Durant-Dort which he had built up to become one of the largest manufacturers in the world of horse-drawn vehicles. It was based in Flint, Michegan, then known as the main carriage-building centre in the United States.

Buick had been started a few years earlier by the Scottish-born David Dunbar Buick. Before long Buick's production of cars under Durant was second only to Henry Ford's famous Model 'T' introduced in 1908, though the Buick was aimed at a more upmarket clientele. Its founder was a talented engineer; his prototype car of 1903 had an engine with valves in the cylinder head and this layout, then rare, was to remain a feature of all later Buick engines. It was also to be characteristic of Chevrolet, Vauxhall and Bedford models of later years.

Interestingly, from 1912 Buicks were sold in Britain with English bodywork as 'all British Bedfords' and then as Bedford Buicks.

By the autumn of 1910 Durant's General Motors which had acquired several other makers, some far less successful, was heading for financial disaster. As a result, Durant stepped down in 1911 and General Motors was run by a consortium of banks.

In October 1911 W. C. Durant started the Little Motor Car Company at the Flint Wagon Works, Michigan. 'The Little' was run by ex-Buick manager William H. Little. A four-cylinder two-seater priced at $650 was produced. Its engine was manufactured by the Mason Motor Company

William C. Durant, founder of General Motors.

which would also manufacture the engine for Chevrolet, Mason being another of the companies owned by Durant.

## LOUIS CHEVROLET

Louis Chevrolet had been born into the family of Joseph Felicien Chevrolet, a Swiss watchmaker, in December 1878. He was one of seven children. The family was poor and when Louis was six years of age they moved from La Chaux-de-Fonds in Switzerland to the ancient Burgundian town of Beaune in France. All the Chevrolet children left school early to find work to help support the family.

However, Louis felt that America was the land of opportunity and together with his younger brothers Arthur and Gaston, crossed the Atlantic to the New World around 1901. They lived for a short period in Quebec and Montreal before moving to New York State. A number of jobs followed, first with a Swiss immigrant by the name of William Walter in Brooklyn. He then joined De Dion Bouton in New York City. From there, Louis moved to the Winton Motor Carriage Company, which would eventually become a division of General Motors producing marine diesel engines. From Winton he moved to Pope-Toledo of Brooklyn and then on to Rambler and Waverley.

**Louis Chevrolet**

In 1904 he joined the FIAT agents Holland Tangeman in New York. The year 1905 saw Louis Chevrolet's fortunes improve as, apart from getting married to Suzanne Trevvoux whom he met the previous winter after she had emigrated from Paris, he also won his first motor racing event. On 20th May, driving a 90hp FIAT at Morris Park, New York, he won by a margin of 52.8 seconds at a speed of 68mph.

Louis Chevrolet became both popular and successful as a racing driver, winning first prize in numerous national events. This success brought him to the attention of several automobile manufacturers. William Crapo Durant, the founder of General Motors, was one of those who had noticed Chevrolet's skills on the track.

During the period 1909-1910 Louis Chevrolet beat the well-known Barney Oldfield, the fastest and probably the best-known American racing driver of his day, on several occasions. Impressed by the racing skills of the Chevrolet brothers, William C. Durant suggested that they should race each other on a track behind the Buick factory at Flint. Louis won the race and was given a place in the Buick racing team. He also did road testing for the firm. Some of the best drivers of the day drove for Buick and Louis Chevrolet found himself rubbing shoulders with the likes of Bob Burman and Louis Strong. Arthur Chevrolet was employed as W. C. Durant's chauffeur.

Louis was an able designer; before joining the Buick team he had successfully modified Buick-based racing cars. Meanwhile he had been thinking of designing a light car of the type that had proved to be very popular in France. In the early Spring of 1911 W. C. Durant bought a garage at 3939 Grand River Avenue, Detroit and Louis Chevrolet was promised financial backing by Durant as a result.

Assisted by Etienne Plache, a fellow countryman whom he had known since his days with Holland and Tangerman in New York, Louis designed two different cars, a four-cylinder and a six-cylinder. The six-cylinder was chosen for production. The model 'C', or Classic Six, was an expensive car of ample proportions, powered by a 4499cc T head engine.

Testing of the new Chevrolet car continued throughout the summer of 1911 and the Chevrolet Motor Company was incorporated on 3rd November 1911. Louis Chevrolet was the consulting engineer with W. H. Little as President. The General Manager was Alexander Hardy. A site for a new factory had been purchased opposite Ford's Highland Park Works, in Detroit, in addition to a garage which was rented on West Grand Boulevard.

The first Chevrolet cost $2,150 and some 2,900 cars had been produced by the end of 1912. The small plant was not very profitable to operate and in 1913 the price of the Classic Six was increased to $2,500.

The relationship between Louis Chevrolet, the engineer, and W. C. Durant, the businessman and entrepreneur, had never been an easy one. Unlike Durant, Chevrolet did not want to compete with Henry Ford. He was also a man of principle. On returning from a trip to France, he was amazed to find that he had not even been told that, as a result of Durant's change of mind, the new Chevrolet factory in Detroit had not been built. Louis Chevrolet thus parted company with Durant in December 1913 telling him, "I sold you my car, I sold you my name but I am not going to sell myself to you."

In later years Louis Chevrolet worked for various enterprises, of which the best-known was the Frontenac Motor Company he started at Indianapolis, making very successful racing cars and the Chevrolet Brothers' manufacturing company, making the Fronty-Ford racing car for Henry Ford. But other ventures collapsed and by 1931, just as the first Bedford vehicles appeared, he became bankrupt. Ironically, he joined the Chevrolet division of General Motors in 1933, as a mechanic.

## DURANT'S CHEVROLET

Meanwhile, W. C. Durant was continuing his policy of building up a chain of manufacturers, from which he could regain his former commanding position. Some were more successful than others but unlike the Chevrolet, Durant's 'Little' car proved to be a profitable proposition. Little's general manager, Alexander Hardy told Durant that in his opinion the name Little was not suitable for an automobile marque. Durant liked the name Chevrolet and after he decided to move all production to Flint in 1913 it was eventually decided to phase out the 'Little' name.

The Little Motor Car Company introduced a six-cylinder 3.6-litre tourer, the 'Little Six' in 1914, but it was a failure and production ceased the following year. The year 1914 also saw the ending of production of the Chevrolet 'Classic Six'. In the same year an important new model was introduced, the H series, designed between August and December 1913. Powered by an OHV four-cylinder engine with exposed pushrods, this tough 2802cc unit was designed by an ex-Buick engineer, Arthur C. Mason, of the Mason Motor Company and would remain in production until 1928. The chassis was the work of another Buick engineer, A. T. Sturt, who did design work for Durant in his spare time.

The Chevrolet Motor Company produced 5,989 vehicles in 1913. By 1915, sales had increased to 13,292. Early in 1915 A. J. Sturt joined the company from Buick in the capacity of chief engineer. Two years earlier the famous Chevrolet 'bow-tie' emblem had been introduced. The design is said to have originated from some wallpaper which lined the walls of W. C. Durant's bedroom whilst he was staying in Paris in 1908.

The H series were available as the Baby Grand tourer and the Royal Mail Roadster. Pleased with Chevrolet's sales, resulting in the marque being placed tenth in that year's sales league, Durant announced further expansion with a view to competing with Ford and Willys.

In October 1915 he incorporated the Chevrolet Motor Company in Delaware as a holding company for all Chevrolet activities. This was the first move in Durant's scheme to take over the General Motors presidency.

By now with plants in Fort Worth, Texas; Toledo, Ohio; St. Louis, Missouri, and Bay City, Michigan, Durant's plans were nearing fulfilment. For five years General Motors shareholders had not received any dividends, since the group's enforced reconstruction in 1910. This was a direct result of Durant's style of management.

Throughout the period between October 1915 and June of the following year, Durant did his best to persuade General Motors stockholders to exchange their shares for those of the promising Chevrolet company. He also increased the capital of the Chevrolet Motor Company of Delaware by $60 million to $80 million. Durant achieved his objective; by May 1916 the Chevrolet Motor Company had acquired 54% of General Motors shares. In the June of the same year Durant was elected President of General Motors. Also a new plant was opened at Oakland, California, the first of its kind on the West Coast. The Delaware Chevrolet Company now owned General Motors!

In October 1915, just as these manoeuvres were beginning, Chevrolet announced the 490 model, that being its price in dollars as a very basic tourer, pitched a little above the then price of the model T Ford. That had steadily come down from the $825 at which it had first appeared in 1908 and in 1915 was selling at $440 in the form nearest to the 490, but specification differences meant that briefly they competed almost head-on. In reality the 490 was a cheaper and smaller version of the H series Baby Grand, sparsely equipped and painted matt black. Chevrolet sales grew, not enough to seriously dent Ford's huge success at that stage, but helping Durant to achieve his objective.

The H series gave way to the largely similar F series in 1917, though the 490 series continued until 1922, at prices never as low as at its introduction. Chevrolet had reached fourth place in the sales league with the 110,839 vehicles produced in 1917, though some uncertainty as to the future followed the entry of the United States into the 1914-18 war that year. A further Chevrolet venture of 1917 was the introduction of the series D, with a 4,719cc Mason-built V8 engine, but it did not live up to expectations and production ceased in 1919. For the next decade, all Chevrolet models had four-cylinder engines and a V8 did not re-appear until 1955.

## GM's CHEVROLET in the USA

In May 1918, General Motors Corporation bought the operating assets of Chevrolet and the Chevrolet Motor Company became a division of General Motors. Even with that late start, its sales figure that year was second only to Buick within the Corporation, and with the war over in November that year, in 1919 it moved into first place, with 117,840 cars and trucks, though Buick was only just behind at that stage at 115,401 and Ford was still much larger.

Also in 1919, the first Chevrolet commercial vehicles were produced, the initial model being a 1-tonner known as the T-series. It had a 3.7-litre engine, with four cylinders and overhead valves, as was to be expected of a Chevrolet of that period; a governor was used to keep the maximum speed down to 25mph. There was a 13-gallon fuel tank under the driver's seat and the wheelbase was 125in.

The price of General Motors stock fell during the Spring of 1920. Durant's run of good fortune was about to change. Realising that he might lose control of General Motors he started buying its shares. In the end, however, he was short of the necessary funds by $1,000,000, with the added difficulty of 300,000 General Motors shares coming up for sale. As it happened, help came from John J Rask of the du Pont Chemical Company who took over Durant's debts with an injection of $20m dollars from du Pont and J. P. Morgan, the banker. On 30th November, 1920, Durant stepped down from the presidency for the last time.

Never one to give up, Durant then started a fresh business, Durant Motors Inc. of New York City, cars being produced under the Star name between 1922 and 1928, but sales were disappointing.

As there was already a strong du Pont holding in General Motors, it was agreed that Pierre S. du Pont be appointed as President of the Corporation in succession to Durant. However, Alfred P. Sloan had become a Director when his Hyatt Roller Bearing Company was acquired by GM in 1918, and even before Durant resigned he had become increasingly influential. In 1923, when Pierre du Pont resigned, Sloan was elected President by the GM Board, continuing in an active role as the Corporation's chief executive officer until 1946. His book 'My years with General Motors' is regarded as a classic account of the management of a huge organisation, as well as revealing as to the basic philosophy adopted by General Motors throughout his period of office.

Circumstances in the United States – great distances, very cheap petrol and often poor roads – generally favoured larger and more robust cars than those sold in large numbers in Europe and this meant that vans and small trucks up to about the 30-cwt (1½ ton) class could be based on car models with little alteration – indeed standard car

chassis could often be used for commercial purposes. Hence the development of the light commercial vehicle and the car were closely bound together, the former benefiting from the economies possible because of the vast sales of cars. In Britain, cars having large engines were heavily penalised by the taxation system based on engine size and thus American developments were apt to be more influential in terms of commercial vehicles.

Alfred P. Sloan summed up the changing pattern of development of the car business in the United States over the earlier years of this century as falling into three periods. He defined that up to 1908 as the 'class market', when cars were expensive and yet relatively unreliable; from 1908 to the mid-1920s as the 'mass market', 'ruled by Ford with his concept of mass transportation at a low dollar price', and then from the mid-1920s as the 'mass-class market', when better standards became available at competitive prices in a market with more diversity.

In 1920, Chevrolet produced 134,117 cars and trucks in the US and Canada, compared to 1,074,336 produced by Ford. The total General Motors output from seven makes was was only a little over a third of this figure, at 393,075, though in money terms GM's net sales at $567 million were not so far short of Ford's $645 million, because the average GM model was much more expensive. Early in 1921, even the cheapest Chevrolet, the 490, with a price that had gone up to $795 for the roadster, came out at $300 more than the Ford T, of which the lowest price had fallen to $395 at that stage.

General Motors had acquired a number of makes, some unprofitable, alongside its standard bearers, Buick and Cadillac, which represented high quality and reliability. The rest of the line, in ascending order of price were Chevrolet, Oakland, Oldsmobile, Scripps-Booth and Sheridan. The last two were "excess baggage" in Sloan's words, soon to be shut and sold off respectively, whilst the introduction by Oakland of the popular Pontiac marque in 1926 lead to the latter's success and the demise of the Oakland line in 1932. There was a slump in 1921, GM slipping in its share of the market and Henry Ford tightening his grip. A committee was set up to consider how to challenge Ford and improve GM's position overall. The plan was to have a more carefully graduated range of cars covering the whole price range, and to develop Chevrolet with models slightly dearer than the Ford T, but offering better value.

The Chevrolet commercial range was rationalised and expanded. In 1921, the larger 3.7-litre engine as used in the T-series, and also used in the FA cars introduced in 1918 and the FB of 1919, was replaced by the 2,802cc unit originally designed for the H series cars of 1914. By 1922, there was also G-series three-quarter ton model with 120in wheelbase and a half-tonner based on the 490 car, with 102in wheelbase.

However, an attempt to exploit new technology misfired, literally – in that a revolutionary Chevrolet known as the 'copper-cooled' model proved unable to run satisfactorily in warm weather – it was actually air-cooled, using copper finned jackets to convey the heat from the cylinders. It taught GM a lesson, that although new ideas could be valuable, they needed to be well proven before being adopted on models in large-scale production. Over the years, many valuable new concepts, often ultimately very widely adopted by vehicle makers on a world scale, have come from General Motors, but almost always they have been thoroughly devloped before being announced and thus very successful.

A further slump in America in 1924 again hit Chevrolet more than Ford. Work was in hand to improved the former's specification, with roomier and better-finished bodywork and, in particular, a stronger rear axle casing to overcome a known weakness, the result being the K-type. In 1925, on a rising market, Chevrolet sold 481,267 cars and trucks, a rise of 64% on the 1924 figure. Ford held even at about 2 million, but its total market share fell from 54% to 45%. Yet in the low price range, the model T Ford seemed very secure, with 70% of the market and the price down even lower to $290 for the tourer. The cheapest Chevrolet at that date was $510, but its specification was better, and the gap was less between saloon models.

The GM plan was to steadily improve specifications in the expectation that Ford would stick to the basic car idea that had served him so well. In 1924-5 there was a marked trend to closed cars in the US and in this GM had a strong advantage with its Fisher body plant, able to supply the huge numbers needed quickly. Alfred Sloan reckoned that the Ford T, with its light chassis, was unsuited to closed bodywork, inevitably heavier, and so taking a lesser share of this key market. In 1926, Chevrolet had about 692,000 US sales and Ford about 1,550,000.

Dramatically, Ford shut his plant in May 1927, not restarting production again until the autumn with the completely new model A. The gap let Chevrolet into the lead, making 940,000 US sales in 1927, the total output going over a million for the first time. It also allowed Walter P. Chrysler, once a GM top executive, who had set up his own business and built it up, notably by acquiring Dodge, to gain a foothold for a third serious competitor in the American low-priced car field, the Plymouth. Thereafter, the General Motors, Ford and Chrysler groups were to be the main competitors for the huge American market, and all three were also to compete for commercial vehicle business in Britain, Chrysler with its Dodge marque.

General Motors' policy of product improvement was more than just a slogan, and as early as 1925, Ormond E. Hunt, Chevrolet's Chief Engineer began work on a new six-cylinder engine to replace the venerable four-cylinder unit on his division's cars and trucks. In December 1928 this, the famous 'stove bolt six', appeared as a 3.2-litre unit in the new range, comprising the series-AC car and light van and the LQ 30-cwt commercial model. Again it had overhead valves, so the old Chevrolet slogan, 'Valves in head, ahead in value' continued to be valid.

## GENERAL MOTORS in the UK

General Motors began to consider expansion into Europe immediately after the 1914-18 war, and in 1919 considered a bid to purchase the Citroen company in France, then a new entrant to the industry but already planning to build 100 cars per day. It decided against proceeding, partly as a result of the attitude of the French government, which was not keen to allow a major French manufacturer to pass into foreign hands.

Buick cars had been marketed in Britain since 1909 and, as already mentioned, were sold as Bedford Buicks for a period from 1912. The market in Britain for imported cars of designs that suited American needs was limited, partly by import duties and partly by the horse-power tax, calculated on a Royal Automobile Club formula related to the bore size of the cylinders and their number, which favoured the use of smaller engines of long-stroke type.

Thus even the modest Ford T, though built in quite large numbers in Britain from 1911 and, briefly in the mid-1920s, actually cheaper to buy than an Austin Seven, suffered from having its 2.88-litre engine rated at 23hp

Ormond E. Hunt, Chief Engineer of Chevrolet and designer of the 'stove bolt six' engine from which the early Bedford engine was developed. He became a Vice-President of GM in 1929.

RAC rating. The four-cylinder Chevrolet was almost as heavily penalised at 22hp. The Buick did rather better, despite being more expensive, having enough prestige to appeal to middle-class tastes.

The problem of import duties was met by importing from Canada which, as an 'Empire' country, gained from Imperial preference, causing most of the Buick cars sold in Britain to come from that concern's McLaughlin factory – another of Durant's purchases – in Canada.

The commercial vehicle position was different, since taxation was related to weight, or in the case of buses, seating capacity, and the rugged yet relatively light construction and low cost, by comparison with British marques built only in small numbers, gave American models quite a strong market here. Numerous American makes appeared on the British market from the early 1920s, and it was decided that Chevrolet models would be assembled at General Motors Ltd's premises in Hendon on the north-western outskirts of London, beginning in 1923. The operation was controlled by Charles Bartlett, who had begun as an accounting clerk at the plant in 1921.

However, General Motors was still interested in purchasing a European manufacturer, and early in 1925 an approach was made to the Austin Motor Company Ltd at Longbridge, Birmingham. That concern, like many on both sides of the Atlantic, had been through a difficult spell, though its output of nearly 12,000 cars in 1924 was substantial by British standards at the time, and climbing, thanks to the very successful Seven and Twelve models.

Although negotiations with Austin continued for seven weeks, no agreement was reached, largely because of difficulties over the way Austin valued its assets. Alfred Sloan recorded a sense of relief when he heard that the GM negotiating team had failed to close the deal, even though he had authorised them to go ahead if satisfied, recording that in his view the Austin plant was physically in poor condition at the time and its management weak – a particularly interesting comment in view of the difficulties Leyland experienced after it took over Austin as a major part of the British Motor Corporation in 1968.

Soon after the Austin deal fell through, an approach was made to purchase Vauxhall Motors Ltd, based at Luton. This concern was much smaller than Austin, producing 1,500 cars per year aimed at a higher-priced sector of the market. Alfred Sloan saw it as in no sense a substitute for Austin, looking at it simply as an experiment in overseas manufacturing, when the deal was agreed in October 1925. The investment was seen as modest, at $2,575,291, or roughly £650,000 at the exchange rate then in force. It was a very different type of concern from any then in the General Motors group in background and outlook and although it was to alter in character following the purchase, it brought with it many talented staff who were to make their mark on GM.

## VAUXHALL MOTORS

The name Vauxhall had its origins in 13th Century Plantagenet England. Fulk le Breant was an unscrupulous mercenary employed in the service of the unpopular King John. He was well rewarded for his efforts on behalf of the king and was made Sheriff of Oxford and Hertford in addition to being granted the Manor of Luton by the grateful monarch.

Being an ambitious social climber he married into the powerful Fitzgerald family and as a result of this acquired property on the south bank of the Thames. The house was known as Fulk's Hall which was corrupted over the years to Foxhall and ultimately, after many generations, to Vauxhall.

During the 17th century the site where one of Fulk le Breant's houses had once been was laid out as Pleasure Gardens. Thackeray extols the virtues of Vauxhall Gardens in Vanity Fair though by his time the place had acquired a slightly unsavoury reputation as the haunt of gamblers, thieves and 'ladies of easy virtue'. The gardens were closed in 1859 and nearby in Wandsworth Road in 1857 a young Scottish engineer, Alexander Wilson, set up in business as the Vauxhall Ironworks taking as the company's badge the Griffin which had once appeared on Fulk Le Breant's coat of arms.

The company produced marine steam engines and Wilson was reasonably successful, obtaining several Admiralty contracts. Unfortunately, like many 19th century steam engineers, he was not particularly good on the accounting side and in 1896 a receiver was called in to help reorganise the company. Wilson's departure was one of the early significant changes, for he left the company that same

year and set up as a consulting engineer in Fenchurch Street, London. The company was restructured with limited liability and changed its title to the Vauxhall Iron Works Co Ltd in 1897.

Wilson had never got involved with the design of motor cars but one of his apprentices, F W Hodges, experimented with a car of continental origin at the turn of the century. The first Vauxhall car was announced in 1903 and by 1904 76 single-cylinder cars had been sold. The following year the company moved to a three-acre site at Luton, Bedfordshire, though this was due to the availability of land at advantageous price and not connected to the award of the Manor of Luton to the erstwhile Fulk le Breant! In the same year a remarkable young man, L. H. Pomeroy, joined the Company. He was a brilliant engineer and in 1912 was made Chief Engineer of Vauxhall Motors, the name of the company after 1907. He was responsible for designing the great vintage Vauxhalls of the years before and after the First World War such as the Prince Henry and the D type which was extensively used as a staff car by the British Army during the war. Probably his greatest achievement was the 30/98, one of the finest of all sports cars, which first appeared in 1913.

Laurence Pomeroy was elected a Director of Vauxhall Motors in 1913, when he was only 30 years old. The following year another gifted engineer who would exert tremendous influence on Vauxhall joined the company. Clarence E. King worked through the 1914-18 war under Pomeroy and took the latter's position when he left for America in 1919. Between 1920 and 1924, Pomeroy was involved with the the Pomeroy car which was noted for its high aluminium content. He was to make his name again in Britain when he became Chief Engineer of the Daimler Company, introducing the famous Double Six car in 1926, becoming Managing Director by 1930.

After Pomeroy's departure, C. E. King, or CEK as he was always known, took charge of the design of new models, including the 14/40, of which about 3,500 were made between 1924 and 1927 – it was the principal product of the factory when General Motors took over. It had a 2,297cc four-cylinder side-valve engine but this had an aluminium cylinder head embodying some of Harry Ricardo's expertise, and although not having anywhere near the performance of the more famous 30/98, was reckoned to be one of the most pleasant cars to drive among comparable models.

After the General Motors takeover, development of existing models did not cease, the 14/40 receiving four-wheel brakes in 1926 and the 30/98, which already had this feature since 1923, moved on to hydraulic operation in 1926, a very advanced feature at that date. A new 3.9-litre six-cylinder model, the 25/70, with Burt-McCullum sleeve valves, also appeared in 1926 but only 50 were made, and this was the last type to be designed before the new owners' influence became apparent.

General Motors at first put an American, Bob Evans, in charge of the factory after the takeover. Capital for expansion and the group's huge technical resources became available, not least in the area of mass production techniques

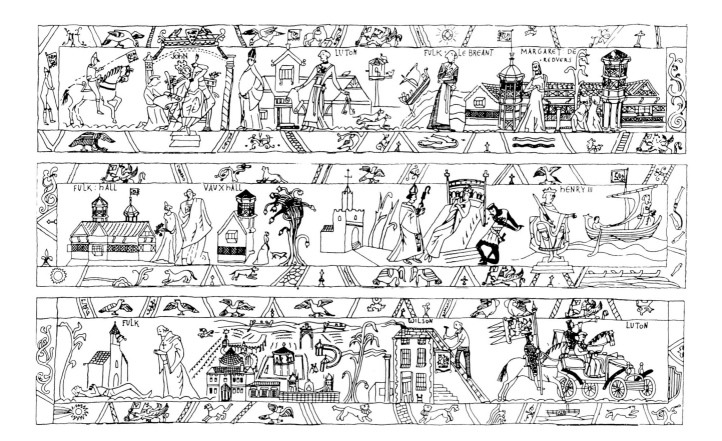

to reduce costs and open up the increased sales which GM sought for its products.

In 1927 the 20/60 or R-type appeared, with six-cylinder overhead-valve 2.76-litre engine, priced at a level lower than the 14/40. It had what were then regarded as transatlantic features such as coil ignition and a centre rather than right-hand gear-change, though the engine itself was derived from previous designs, with pressure-fed seven main bearing crankshaft. Some of the traditionalists were unhappy but sales were up. The company's interest in the Bedford name recurred as one of the saloon body types was called the Bedford, though this rather suggests that at that stage its use for a new goods range may not yet have been in mind.

In fact, there was strong continuity, most notably in regard to C. E. King, who continued as Chief Engineer, and in the words of his son, the late Geoffrey King, "he invited fellow engineers who were already with the company in 1925 to join in tackling the problems that lay ahead".

In his book, Alfred Sloan commented that Vauxhall lost money in the first few years after GM took it over, and it gradually became clear that a smaller car would have to be developed if it was hoped to capture a much larger share of the British Market. It was also very significant that in 1930, on Sloan's advice, Bob Evans was replaced as Managing Director by Charles Bartlett, who had been in charge of the Chevrolet assembly work at the Hendon factory. The GM President thought that an Englishman

**A lighthearted though quite accurate rendering of the origins of the Vauxhall name, beginning with the changing fortunes of Fulk le Brent, done rather in the manner of the Bayeaux tapestry. It may have been no more than coincidental that Vauxhall took up a local name with medieval origins, but Vauxhall Motors was a typically British company and, although part of General Motors from 1925 and governed thereafter by its decisions, it developed a distinctive character of its own, not least in its Bedford commercial vehicles.**

should be in charge of an English factory.

For the first few years of the new regime, the assembly of Chevrolet models, goods and passenger, continued at Hendon quite independently of the GM-owned Vauxhall factory at Luton, which continued to have no involvement with commercial vehicles. This continued until 1929, the first examples of the new six-cylinder series AC, available in car form or as a 12-cwt light delivery model, and the series LQ 30-cwt, still being assembled at Hendon.

For reasons already explained, the Chevrolet car, even in this much improved form, had only a limited market in Britain, but the commercial models, particularly the LQ, became an almost instant success, becoming a far more familiar sight all over Britain in lorry, van and small bus forms than the earlier types. The logic of moving to new premises on the Vauxhall site at Luton was clear, and the AC and LQ models were assembled at Luton from 1929 to 1931, latterly being described as the Chevrolet Bedford models and thus helping to tie in their identity with the first Bedford chassis when this first appeared in April 1931.

# 2 ASSEMBLING THE TEAM

The purchase of Vauxhall Motors by General Motors in November 1925 provided the means to manufacture, as opposed merely to assemble, the promising Chevrolet commercial vehicles in Britain. First requirements were to establish a talented team to develop and improve the Chevrolet models for the British and Empire market and this task fell to C. E. King, Vauxhall's Chief Engineer.

Comparison of Chevrolet and early Bedford models confirms the great similarity of design although clearly the opportunity had been taken to update and improve where necessary or desirable. The new team would naturally have made improvements and whilst the most fundamental of these concerned the engine's lubrication system – mentioned later – there were many smaller but nevertheless significant changes.

Several of the men who joined the new Vauxhall organisation, after General Motors took over in 1925, came from Rolls Royce, Sunbeam, Cadillac and in the case of P. Stepney Acres, Napier. It was therefore to be expected that engineering standards would be high. The reputation for engineering leadership was a major factor in the success of the Bedford.

Whilst the great engineers who were responsible for this success are regrettably almost unknown to the average commercial motoring enthusiast, the author is fortunate in having learned of them from the late Geoffrey King, son of C. E. King. Geoffrey worked under his father at Luton for several years and knew many of the team which had made Bedford the United Kingdom's leading commercial vehicle manufacturer and revived the fortunes of the Vauxhall company.

Over many cups of coffee and talk of the 'days before yesterday' at Luton, this book was born. Sadly, Geoffrey passed away in July 1989, having suffered from leukaemia for several years. His knowledge of the pre- and early post-war years at Luton was invaluable in the preparation of this book.

## C. E. King

CEK's strong principles, which would eventually guide the Vauxhall and Bedford marques to such success throughout the 'thirties and 'forties, were probably inherited from his father who was an early Socialist – an upholsterer by trade. His principles, however, did not always correspond with his employers' requirements. Because of this he frequently changed his employment, moving home some eleven times in fourteen years.

CEK was born in the Highbury Hill district of north London and attended the local elementary school in Clapham Road. By the time he was in his middle teens his father was living at the Anglers' Rest public house just outside Bedford.

Around this time CEK joined the local Adams Manufacturing Company Ltd at Bedford, makers of the Adams motor car between 1905 and 1914. Initially he worked as a mechanic but was given charge of the drawing office in December 1911. During this period, like many other gifted mechanically-minded young men, CEK studied at night school.

From surviving references written at the time by the chief draughtsman and the managing director, CEK was thought of as a most capable draughtsman, being both quick and accurate. On 26th May 1912 he terminated his employment with Adams Cars, having decided some time earlier to further his other interest in life, that of painting.

By 1912 King was a member of the Independent Labour Party in Bedford, which was considered very avant-garde at the time. It was at the ILP that he met his future wife with whom he travelled to Paris after leaving Adams in 1912.

CEK had moderate success as a painter and several members of his family had also dabbled in drawing and painting in an amateur way. He lived in a proverbial garret on the Rue Campagne Premier. In latter years he would tell his family how, during those months in 1912, he lived on bread and golden syrup, except when he could cadge a meal from richer friends !

During this period CEK had been in correspondence with the Société Lorraine and received a reply dated 26th August 1912, more or less offering him a job as a draughtsman. His son Geoffrey told me he took the job because "Mother liked to eat regularly." Just before joining Société Lorraine he got married, the wedding taking place at the British Consulate in Paris.

As the war clouds gathered over Europe, CEK wrote to Vauxhall Motors requesting a job in the drawing office and returned to England with his wife, joining Vauxhall Motors in 1914.

Throughout the First World War period he worked under L. H. Pomeroy, the Chief Engineer and, in 1919, on Pomeroy's departure to America, took over his position.

In 1923 the OE type 30/98 was introduced, the engine of which was an overhead valve unit designed by CEK. By this time his salary was twelve hundred pounds a year, rising to fifteen hundred pounds a year in 1924, the last year of the Vauxhall company's independence. Clarence E. King remained chief engineer until 1952 and retired from the Board in 1954. During his 33 years as Chief

C. E. King, Chief Engineer of Vauxhall Motors from 1919 to 1952. His term of office included the whole of the formative years of Bedford described in this volume.

Harold Drew, Assistant Chief Engineer, 1929-53, one of several notable engineers joining Vauxhall after the General Motors takeover

Maurice Olley (left) and Alex Taub, seen soon after they joined Vauxhall's engineering team in 1937, both from other parts of the GM empire though with a British background.

Engineer the vehicles produced by Vauxhall Motors gained a world-wide reputation for engineering excellence.

## C. J. Bartlett

If C. E. King was the architect of the post-General Motors Engineering philosophy at Luton, then Charles John Bartlett was the architect of the far-sighted industrial relations policy and a brilliant Managing Director.

Bartlett was Gloucestershire-born, into a modest west country family. After leaving school he attended Bath Technical College where he trained in business methods, specialising in accountancy. During the First World War he fought with the Devonshire Regiment, which he joined in 1914. By the end of the war Charles Bartlett had reached the rank of sergeant. During the early part of the war he was wounded at the battle of Loos and later served in the Middle East. Charles Bartlett was a countryman at heart, with an interest in farming and horticulture. He was a man with a robust and democratic approach to industrial management. This was combined with a sense of humour and a strong will; a determination to provide not only a better working environment but to break down the barriers which had caused so many problems at the workplace.

His rise to the heights at Vauxhall was, to say the least, spectacular. In 1921 he had been an accounting clerk; in 1923 he was placed in charge of the Hendon assembly plant and by 1930 he had become Managing Director of Vauxhall Motors Ltd.

Another of Bartlett's great contributions to the industry and to industrial democracy in this country was his Management Advisory Committee, set up in 1941. The factory was split up into twenty areas; a representative for each area was elected by secret ballot, and the representatives of the Management Advisory Committee met Charles Bartlett every four weeks to discuss outstanding problems. After a three-year term the representatives automatically retired but were eligible for re-election together with six management representatives.

This whole concept of management was in total contrast to many of the company's rivals, whose industrial relations policies often left much to be desired. The lack of industrial disputes during Bartlett's period was a direct result of his enlightened management.

Assisting King and Bartlett was an extremely talented group of people, some of the more prominent of whom are listed below.

## R. Evans

During the early years of GM ownership Vauxhall had been run by an American, Bob Evans. Evans was an expert in the art of shaping sheet steel. He built and equipped a press shop and die shop at Luton and personally instructed skilled men in the use of machinery and hand finishing to obtain a perfect draw. He was replaced in 1930 to allow C. J. Bartlett to run Vauxhall Motors Ltd.

## P. Stepney Acres

Vauxhall Motors was blessed with an extremely talented commercial vehicle designer. P. Stepney Acres joined the company in 1927 from Napier, a company whose motor car designs during the earlier years of this century rivalled Rolls Royce in their excellence of design and general refinement.

If the first Bedfords to leave Luton were nothing more than improved Chevrolets with full-pressure lubrication, then the brilliant WT model announced in the November of 1933 and available to operators from June of the following year was the first truly original design and its success owed much to Stepney Acres' forward thinking.

Acres was a fine mathematician and like several other members of the Luton team, was a strong personality. I well remember my late friend Geoffrey King remarking how Acres on one hand was not above using strong language when he thought the occasion demanded it and yet would thoroughly enjoy an evening at Covent Garden. Stepney Acres was assisted by R. R. Bishop.

## H. Drew

During the 1930s and for many years after, Bedford commercial vehicles and Vauxhall cars were powered by engines which were unsurpassed in their respective fields. The original Bedford engines were developed by ex-Sunbeam engineer Harold Drew who had been encouraged to join the motor industry by Malcolm Campbell. His first job was in Wolverhampton as an engineering draughtsman with the famous Sunbeam company, working under the direction of Louis Coatalen.

In 1925 Drew left Sunbeam and joined General Motors to carry out engineering assignments in Europe. Later he moved to Oldsmobile as a draughtsman before joining Vauxhall in the latter half of 1927 and, in 1929 became assistant chief engineer under C. E. King, a position he held until 1953.

## A. Taub

In 1937 Drew, Vauxhall's engine designer, was joined by Alex Taub. Taub was born into a Jewish working class family in the East End of London, which was employed in the fur trade. He was fortunate in that he had wealthy relations living in America and it was these who paid for the greater part of his education in the United States. Alex Taub worked originally for Chevrolet under Ormond Hunt and was involved in the design of the six-cylinder Chevrolet engine of 1929, often referred to in later years as the 'cast iron wonder' and the 'stove bolt six'.

During the early 'thirties Taub was responsible for a series of four main bearing experimental Chevrolet engines (as opposed to the usual three main bearing design), which resulted in the introduction of an improved and updated design from Chevrolet in 1937.

As a result of the completion of his experiments and design studies Chevrolet were able to release Taub to Luton to continue his work in furthering the design of the internal combustion engine.

In recent years there has been a lot of discussion about lean burn combustion. Alex Taub was interested in such ideas in the 'thirties. As a result Vauxhall-Bedford engines often gave excellent fuel consumption figures, one of the best examples being the company's four-cylinder 10hp (RAC) engine introduced in 1937; 40mpg was quite easily obtainable.

Taub is also remembered for the uninhibited manner in which he taught some War Office die-hards the principles of engine lubrication and carburettor design when, during the first Winter of the Second World War, army vehicle engines refused to turn over in the exceptionally cold weather due to the excessively heavy oil specified by the authorities.

He was a very direct man and could at times be extremely outspoken. His contribution to engine design generally is probably greatly underestimated. Certainly his later achievements, at the beginning of the Second World War, played a significant part in the Allies' victory over the Axis powers.

## M. Olley

Maurice Olley originally joined Cadillac from Rolls Royce where he had worked with Henry Royce. He moved to Vauxhall in 1937, by which time he was well known for his expertise on suspension systems, steering and transmissions.

Because of his studies at Cadillac the General Motors Corporation adopted independent front suspension for all car divisions in the mid-'thirties. His paper on the subject which was presented to the Society of Automotive Engineers in 1934 was noted for its clarity of exposition.

Both Olley and Taub had a great influence upon design and engineering at Vauxhall Motors.

## M. Platt

Maurice Platt joined Vauxhall Motors in mid-1937, being already well-known to the firm as a technical journalist, having first met C. E. King when visiting the Luton premises for *The Motor* in 1924. He was invited to join the company by Charles Bartlett, and worked successively for Maurice Olley and Alex Taub, whose responsiblities in regard to the Churchill tank engine he took over in 1940. The large-scale supply of trucks to the Army led to the development of rough-track testing during the war, and paved the way for this to be used in the development of post-war models. After the war his responsibilities switched to cars but in 1953 he succeeded C. E. King as Chief Engineer.

## G. H. Hutchings

G. H. Hutchings worked under C. E. King and was in charge of public service vehicle design. Hutchings was responsible for the famous Bedford bus and coach chassis designs such as the WTB and the OB.

## D. Jones

Styling for many years at Luton, under the guidance of Harley Earl's famous styling team at General Motors, was in the hands of David Jones RA who originally joined Vauxhall Motors in 1934 and stayed on into the 1960s. Body design on both commercial vehicle cabs and motor cars was the responsibility of Tony Cooke who came to Luton from Rolls Royce in 1937.

* * * * * * * * *

Other members of the design team included H. A. Dean, a premium apprentice when he joined the firm in 1919, who later became assistant service manager, and Frank Gibson. Both were experimental engineers, Frank Gibson having started in this capacity under Pomeroy in 1919. Bob Weston, who became the chief draughtsman, worked for the company for 45 years, having sought a job at Vauxhall after hearing a talk given by Pomeroy in 1913. Clearly the company engendered loyalty and long service from its key employees.

# 3 THE BRITISH CHEVROLET

## Assembly at Hendon

The American-built 10-cwt Chevrolet had found a market in the UK, but the 1-ton British market was completely dominated by Ford in the early 'twenties. General Motors recognised this and decided to exploit the opportunity and to compete with Ford head on by introducing a one-tonner for British users and assembling it in Hendon, London thereby avoiding import duty on the complete vehicle.

Manufacture of the chassis components continued in Canada but a new factory was created at The Hyde, Hendon, on the Edgware Road in North London, an area which was being transformed from farm land into industrial development. Assembly of Chevrolet vehicles for the British market began there in early 1923 and the first sale was recorded in June of that year, this being a 1-ton lorry registered CD 7912, for a Mr C Jenking of Brighton.

The UK operation was controlled by Charles Bartlett and his success may be measured by his rise from being an accounting clerk with General Motors Ltd, Hendon, in 1921 to becoming Managing Director of Vauxhall Motors nine years later.

American practices were, naturally, introduced and in the report of a visit to the new factory in June 1923 *The Commercial Motor* noted that the widespread use of jigs coupled with standardised manufacture of components meant that assembly was carried out by unskilled labour. The factory was well-equipped and well laid out, including such advanced techniques as vacuum removal of dust from the saw mill.

A complete chassis, including electrics, cost £190 which was seen as very competitive. Plans were already in hand for the provision of bodywork and the cost of a cab with fixed sides and tailboard was quoted as £230 whilst a 14-seater bus cost £380. At this stage many of these bodies would almost certainly have been produced by outside suppliers. A rural bus was advertised in 1924 but clearly this was not the direction the company needed to take if it was to achieve volume production.

In 1925 the decision was taken that production should be standardised on two types of van body. The factory was tooled up and eight 10-cwt vans and ten 1-ton lorry bodies were being produced daily by 1926, with a total workforce of 100 including clerical staff. The company was proud to be able to state that other than supervisory staff no skilled labour was employed, such was the quality of its manufacture and the effectiveness of its jig assembly. *The Commercial Motor* reporter recorded when he toured the factory in July 1926 that 'not a chisel was in sight', an unusual situation in most British coachbuilding factories at that time .

Master patterns were produced and issued to the sawmill chargehand for batch production as required. Considerable investment in plant had taken place and multiple machining was commonplace. These were the means by which GM was able to bring down the price of the vehicles.

Assembly took place on a production line with manufactured components stored alongside the line for immediate availability as required. Metal components were manufactured to the same rigid tolerances and the company was also proud to state that it had completely eliminated blacksmith's work. The cost of a cab, trimmed and painted, was £22, whilst a complete 1-ton dropside body cost £40.

Work continued on the updating and improvement of the chassis and the Chevrolet became a strong competitor to Ford although from 1924 Chevrolet's main competitor

The first sale of a Chevrolet 1-ton model in Britain, following the beginning of assembly of this model at Hendon in 1923, was of this vehicle, registered CD 7912, to C. Jenking, a landscape gardener based in Brighton, on 30th June that year. It was used largely to carry turf, trees, shrubs, earth, stone for paths, etc to a country estate well off any main road and involving some rough going. Its first duty each morning was to take six or seven men from Brighton to the estate and at the end of the day would bring them back. It was still in use in July 1929.

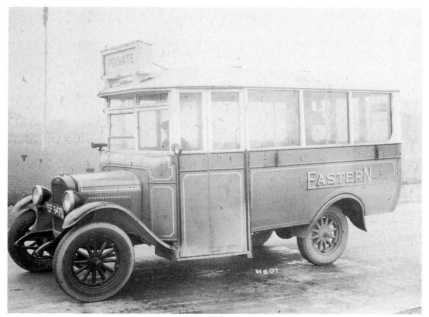

Bus bodywork was fitted to some Chevrolet four-cylinder chassis, though not on the same scale as was to apply later with the LQ type. This example, registered EF 3470, one of a batch of LM models with Strachan & Brown 14-seat bodywork, had been operated from 1927 by Eastern Express Motors Ltd, of West Hartlepool, a company which was acquired by the London & North Eastern Railway and run as a subsidiary until agreements with the Northern General Transport Co Ltd and United Automobile Services Ltd led to its fleet being split in 1930 between those operators. This one, however, was part-exchanged before that happened, with AEC against new vehicles, probably a fleet of Reliance models acquired in 1929, and is seen on a gloomy day at AEC's Southall works. W. E. Brown, who was the Brown of Strachan & Brown, parted company with that organisation in 1928 to take charge of the sales side at Duple, later to become strongly associated with Bedford as its main supplier of passenger bodywork.

in Britain was the 1-ton Morris Commercial using the engine and gearbox from the Morris Oxford car. Amongst arrangements for modifying chassis was an interesting one with the Danish company Longframe Six-wheeler Construction Co to lengthen the chassis and thereby increase the payload to two tons by the provision of a third axle.

By 1928 the Hendon operation had been expanded to produce a wider variety – four separate lines were producing 10 cwt and 20-25 cwt vans, 20-25 cwt cabs and 20-25 cwt drop side bodies. In all cases bodies were completed before being mounted on the finished chassis.

The success of the operation encouraged GM to expand its facilities and accordingly during 1929/30 production was transferred to a new factory at Luton on the Vauxhall site which GM had acquired with that company in 1925.

The Hendon factory continued to be used for many years for modification and special work, and the GM test area where all vehicles were checked and tested remained there.

The next move proved to be the decisive one, however, for the introduction of the LQ range in 1929 enabled General Motors to conquer the British commercial vehicle market thanks to the new model with its lively six-cylinder engine. The move to Luton had come just at the right time to allow the company to capitalise on the demand for its new models, but also to consider the whole future of the UK operation.

## Advent of the LQ range

The Chevrolet as marketed in Britain from 1923 to 1928 had been built in quite a number of variations, but the basic feature they had in common was the four-cylinder overhead-valve engine, with cylinder dimensions of $3^{11}/_{16}$in bore and 4in stroke, giving a 2,802cc capacity – its RAC rating was 21.7 hp. There were three main bearings and the big ends relied on a splash lubrication system, picking up oil from troughs into which they dipped.

Competition over that period was intense but four-cylinder Chevrolet vans and lorries of up to 25-cwt capacity were assembled at Hendon in large numbers and the chassis was also used on a more modest scale for buses in the 14-seat class.

The final examples of this sequence of models were called the National types, in 1928. They were offered in the Series AB 10-cwt form, with a wheelbase of 107in, and the LP 25-cwt model with 124in wheel base. There was a three-speed gearbox on the AB, later LP models having a four-speed unit, and four-wheel brakes, though this latter was then a new feature standardised only on the final series of four-cylinder models. At the rear, the foot brake was of the external-contracting type, the hand brake operating internal-expanding shoes, drivers being advised to use both foot and hand brakes if need be for an emergency stop.

The six-cylinder Chevrolet models introduced in December 1928 marked a major landmark in development, as well as laying the foundation of the early Bedford. They were known as the International series (not to be confused with the completely unrelated International trucks made by the International Harvester Co of Chicago). There were two models, the AC, which was the car version, much as sold in immense numbers in the United States, the same basic chassis also being used as the light delivery model, now rated at 12 cwt, and the LQ, the 30-cwt model. The AC had the same wheelbase as the AB, but the LQ was of 131in (10ft 11in).

Both had the new engine, often nicknamed the 'cast iron wonder' or the 'stove bolt six', of $3^5/_{16}$in bore and 3¾in stroke, giving a capacity of 3,180cc and an RAC rating of 26.33hp, which for the car version brought it into the 27hp taxation rating and virtually killed its sales potential in this form in Britain. The power output was 44bhp at 2,400rpm, quite modest in relation to its size, even by contemporary standards, but the emphasis was on low-speed torque. It had a three-bearing crankshaft and

### 30-cwt. MEAT VAN

Lined Plymax and zinc. All corners rounded. Heavy ash racks on floor. Full width doors and tail-board design for easy loading. Approved by the Medical Health Authorities of Smithfield Market.

**£260**

### 30-cwt. BOX VAN

A smart, strong, capacious van with handsome roof and body lines. Full width doors at rear make for quick and easy loading ; all goods carried can easily be reached. Driver's cab fully enclosed, with two doors and winding glass windows. Adjustable bucket type seats. Detachable partition behind driver supplied as extra equipment.

**£235**

### 30-cwt. LORRY WITH TILT

Sides and tail-board easily detachable. Improved heavy canvas waterproof tilt detachable so that vehicle can be used as open lorry when tilt is not required. Comfortable enclosed cab with winding glass windows.

**£219**

### CHEVROLET 12-cwt. VAN

Full width folding doors at the rear make loading quick and easy. Driver's cab fully enclosed, with two doors with winding glass windows. Sliding bucket seats adjustable for leg room. Additional partition behind driver supplied as extra equipment.

Price, including spare tyre, **£175**

### FOURTEEN-SEATER OMNIBUS

A handsome one-man operated bus, well planned for comfort and convenience. Front entrance door controlled by driver. Rear emergency door. Spring frame seats. Windows adjustable for ventilation. Four interior roof lights and step light.

**£390**

### TWO-STRETCHER AMBULANCE

One or two doors at rear to choice, with frosted glass light and folding step. Stretcher fixtures on one side and accommodation for sitting cases and attendants on the other. Detachable cushions, splint box and water-bottle fitted.

**£335**

An indication of the variety of body types offered is given by this page reproduced from a Chevrolet brochure. The 12-cwt van was on the AC chassis also used for the car version, the others on the LQ. The general appearance of the cabs and van bodies continued into the early Bedford models

The Chevrolet LQ became popular as a 14-seat bus in Britain when introduced in 1929. In those days, before the introduction of the system of road service licencing arising from the Road Traffic Act 1930, a small nimble vehicle had not dissimilar appeal to that of the minibus in today's deregulated circumstances. This one, registered WX 836, and with bodywork by Charles Roberts of Wakefield, was operated by Violet Coaches in the Kippax area of the West Riding of Yorkshire. Note the way in which the single rear wheels were deeply recessed into the mudguards, very typical of small buses of the time.

Another typical Chevrolet LQ was this example, VF 6943, with body built at its Lowestoft works by United Automobile Services Ltd. It was supplied to W. Hammond, trading as Caston Motor Services, of Caston, near Attleborough, Norfolk, being first registered on 14th September 1929 – it was in a maroon and primrose livery. Note the characteristic Chevrolet rear light unit just above the rear number plate. In this case, the seating capacity was 16, and a roof-mounted luggage carrier was provided.

At that date, United had just come into the Tilling & British Automobile Traction group, and bodybuilding work for independent operators was soon to be scaled down before that company's own services in East Anglia, and the coachworks, were handed over to the newly-formed Eastern Counties Omnibus Co Ltd in 1931. The bodybuilding activities became a separate subsidiary, Eastern Coach Works Ltd, in 1936.

area of the operator.

The decision to transfer production to Luton enabled both that the parts were to be of British origin, largely made within the factory, and for manufacture of the engine and the complete chassis to be on true assembly-line methods. New premises were built within the Vauxhall Motors factory site, the work beginning during 1929. The 1930 edition of the instruction book for the model refers to it as 'Luton-built' and it appears that output of completed chassis began during that year. At that stage, no reference in publicity or press reports was made to Vauxhall involvement, the address for business purposes remaining as General Motors Ltd, Edgware Road, The Hyde, Hendon, London N.W.9. Completed vehicles were delivered back to Hendon for testing.

*The Commercial Motor* of 19th August that year included a road test report on what was described as a 'Chevrolet Luton-built Utility 30-cwt lorry', the heading referring to it being manufactured 'at the Luton Works of General Motors Ltd'. The chassis price remained at £190,

the complete vehicle with dropside body being £220. Mention is made of various improvements introduced since the model had been introduced, such as a larger engine oil pump, self-energising front brakes and, in particular on Luton-built chassis, a heavier-duty rear axle, of similar design to the original, but with stronger casing, differential gears and half-shafts. The wheels also became of normal bolt-on type, though still of the characteristic disc type.

The vehicle weighed 1 ton 8 cwt 3 qr and was running at 3 tons with test load and crew. Acceleration from rest to 50mph was quoted at 57 seconds 'not employing first gear'. Present-day car drivers may not find this too impressive, but many commercial vehicles of that time could not have reached 50mph at all, let alone produce a recordable acceleration time. To anyone with experience of the model or early Bedfords, the exclusion of first gear is not surprising, since it was *very* low – General Motors had an edict, still in force in much later days with Bedford, that all its products must be able to climb 1 in 4 fully laden.

A version of the Chevrolet aimed at the hire or hotel trade was this seven-seat landaulette model having a glass partition, folding hood at the rear and roof-mounted luggage rack. It was based on the same AC-type chassis as the car version and was priced at £330, with was £90 more than the standard saloon, doubtless reflecting the cost of a coachbuilt body. The basic body design was not far removed from that of a contemporary London taxi, a line of business pursued briefly a little later with a Bedford version which probably looked very similar although seemingly the project did not go into production.

The LQ model was widely used as a van, this example being operated by the drapery department of the rather splendidly-named Pathhead and Sinclairtown Reform Co-operative Society Ltd of Kirkaldy.

(Indeed, in 1930, a Chevrolet Bedford model climbed Prestatyn Mountain, near Rhyl, in North Wales, which involved a 1 in 3 gradient.) Equally revealing in the test report was the quoting of minimum top-gear speed as 2mph, which speaks volumes for the engine's flexible performance, quite important when driver instruction was minimal. Average fuel consumption worked out at 17.6mpg.

By the time the 1931 edition of the instruction book was printed, the model was being described as the Chevrolet Bedford model – subtly, the transition was under way.

Very possibly the largest user of Chevrolet LQ buses in Britain was the Lincolnshire Road Car Co Ltd. Over 50 are known to have been purchased new in the 1929-31 period, including the 1929 example shown, and others were taken over with acquired businesses. Note the operator's nameplate on the radiator. Many had 20-seat bodywork despite retaining the standard single-tyred rear wheels, although at least two had been converted to six-wheeled layout, also used by various other operators, both passenger and goods. Lincolnshire had been formed in August 1928 to take over an existing business, and in 1929 the LNER and LMS railways acquired interests, followed by the Tilling & British Automobile Traction group, and in later years Leyland vehicles tended to be favoured.

# 4 THE FIRST BEDFORDS

The precise reasons for the choice of the Bedford name for the new goods models produced by Vauxhall Motors were not recorded at the time, even boardroom minutes giving no clue. As indicated in earlier chapters, it had been used for previous products, notably the Bedford-Buick exercise of 1912 in which the Buick car was given an at least partly spurious British identity by being claimed to be 'built' by the Bedford Motor Company based in Willesden, London. Vauxhall had also used the name for body types for its cars – it was quite common practice among makers to use county or town names for the various styles offered.

In addition, it may have been thought best to have a separate name for the commercial vehicles produced by a famous car maker, and again this was common practice, it being reasoned in an age more class-conscious than today that car buyers would not want to have their purchase associated with 'trade'.

Whatever the reason, 'Bedford' was an appropriate choice with a good ring to it, and it very soon became familiar to millions as the name on vehicles to be seen on almost every street.

The first Bedford models appeared in April 1931, in the form of a pair of 2-ton models. It was obvious even to the most casual observer that they bore a close affinity to the

Announcing
*the*
BEDFORD
2-TON TRUCK
LONG & SHORT WHEELBASE
*(Full particulars on following pages)*

Made *by* Vauxhall Motors Ltd.

This was how the new Bedford 2-ton models were presented in the April 1931 edition of General Motors News (London). The front view would have seemed familiar to Chevrolet users since all but the detail styling of the radiator was virtually identical to the LQ. The bold lettering ascribing manufacture to Vauxhall Motors Ltd was noteworthy – the link was rarely stressed as strongly in later years.

The Bedford radiator badge made the Vauxhall link more subtly, using the Griffin emblem as adopted by Vauxhall and with a history going back to Fulk le Brent and the 13th century. Note the use of the words 'Made in England'.

Chevrolet LQ, with very similar general appearance. Moreover the engine was of the same size and outwardly very similar design, and even the wheelbase of the shorter model, the WHG, was the same 131in (10ft 11in) as the LQ – the longer WLG had a wheelbase of 157in (13ft 1in). But to dismiss them as rebadged Chevrolets would be quite wrong, for there were important differences.

Vauxhall's strong engineering team had begun to influence the product going out over its name – at that stage, and for many years, Bedford was no more than a sales name, the maker being quoted as Vauxhall Motors Ltd, Luton, Bedfordshire, though some early references also included The Hyde, Hendon, as an alternative address and initially sales of Bedford models were handled by Chevrolet dealers, though quite soon it was normal for Vauxhall car dealers to also cover Bedford commercial vehicles.

It is not difficult to imagine the culture shock that must have been experienced after Vauxhall came under General Motors control, and especially when production of the Chevrolet LQ had come to Luton. Cleverly designed as it was, the Chevrolet was aimed at the low-priced mass market, whereas Vauxhall had been a car maker aiming at a middle- to upper-class market – even the 14/40 had cost £395 for the chassis alone in 1927, and the 30/98, still revered among car enthusiasts today, had been £950 in chassis form, comparable to the Bentley to which it was a worthy rival.

Yet it is not difficult to see the General Motors viewpoint, as Vauxhall's old ways had led to financial problems and ultimately its sale. However, the development of a 2-ton model derived from the Chevrolet required at least a degree of redesign, and in particular a new rear axle where almost all the extra load would be carried. Twin rear wheels were required but the whole unit was altered, a noteworthy point being the adoption of fully floating design, with the half-shafts relieved of all load-carrying stress, a feature not at that stage found on some much heavier-duty Leyland or AEC models – the visible part of

The first touches of the Bedford 2-tonner's own identity became evident in the side views, with the perforated disc wheels, the larger rear hub and the option of a longer wheelbase evident in the WLG shown in the upper view. The bonnet louvres extended for the full length of the side panel and were less fine than on the Chevrolet, though the WLG prototype seems to have an interim version. The detail views focus on the rear axle – called the back axle in the captions in a down-to-earth way – which was where some of Vauxhall's own engineering had been applied. Note that a spare wheel was provided, but lacking a tyre.

The original Bedford 26.33hp six-cylinder engine as introduced in 1931 was visually very similar to the Chevrolet 'stovebolt six' or 'cast-iron wonder', and having a similarly neat appearance that looks far more modern than most light commercial vehicle engines of the period. The key elements that distinguished the Bedford unit were hidden – full pressure lubrication and a four-main-bearing crankshaft. Accessibilty was excellent in the early chassis – in this off-side view of a restored example, the distributor is in the centre of the picture, with the sparking plugs protected by neat rubber covers. The AC mechanically-driven fuel pump with glass filter bowl is low on the engine side towards the front, with the fuel pipe going round the front of the engine to the carburettor, which was mounted below the manifolds on the other side. The Delco-Remy starter is just behind the steering column. It would be simple to work on any of these items, and tappet adjustment was similarly a matter of undoing the two nuts securing the rocker cover to remove it and reach the adjusting screws on the rockers.

the rear hub thus becoming larger in diameter than on the LQ. The wheels for this model were of the perforated disc type, and various other chassis items, from the frame upwards, were of revised design to suit the additional weight, or in the case of the WLG, extra length. Even so, much remained unaltered, including such items as the petrol tank, mounted under the driver's and passenger's seat. It seems probable that many parts would be interchangeable and, as the Chevrolet AC and LQ were to remain in production at Luton for a further year alongside the Bedford, this would be helpful in manufacture as well as from a spares viewpoint.

Possibly the most significant difference related to the engine. In general specification, it followed the LQ quite closely; the same $3^5/_{16}$in bore and $3\frac{3}{4}$in stroke, 3,180cc capacity and 26.33hp RAC rating – even the quoted power was the same 44bhp at 2,400rpm. In general, it was a close derivative of the Ormond Hunt 'cast iron wonder' design, on which Alex Taub had worked. Yet an important change had been made for the Bedford version, the adoption of full-pressure lubrication feeding main and big-end bearings. There were also four main bearings instead of the three on the Chevrolet unit.

It would be interesting to know what high-level discussions between Vauxhall and GM had taken place, for Chevrolet were to remain faithful to the splash lubrication system for many years, with considerable

This 1932 WHG model owned by Mr O. Clarke of Porth spent five months carrying sewer pipes for the Rhondda Valley drainage scheme, negotiating the rocky bed of the River Taff to carry them into position, as seen here. Note the absence of rear mudgurds, quite common at the time. The bodywork of KG 776 was showing signs of the hard treatment, the rear view revealing how it was sagging under the load imposed on that end.

success, it has to be said. It may have been argued that the extra loading on the 2-ton model's engine, especially if drivers took full advantage of the engine's willingness to pull at low speeds, might be courting disaster if not altered.

Yet it does not need much imagination to visualise C. E. King, as Vauxhall's Chief Engineer, and designer of the engine in the later 30/98, and also Harold Drew, his deputy, with a Sunbeam background, being affronted at the thought of having a splash-lubricated engine going out in products for which they were responsible.

Be that as it may, the original Bedford engine was both popular with drivers and gained a good reputation for reliability. It is particularly interesting to find that the pressure lubrication system – in reality, the key feature that established the separate identity of the Bedford engine – was not even mentioned in contemporary publicity on the new model, doubtless so as not to draw attention to this difference from the Chevrolet, still in production and being sold alongside the Bedford.

The whole chassis was of simple and robust design, the

For the first year, the Chevrolet LQ continued to be sold alongside the new Bedford models, both being built at Luton and the LQ dealing with the 30-cwt business, for which Bedford at first offered no contender. This picture of an LQ appeared in joint publicity covering both makes for the the 1931 Commercial Motor Show, held at Olympia in November of that year. The dropside body was provided with alternative sets of fittings to enable it to be used for different purposes, in this case extending the sides and headboard upwards. The vehicle was priced at £212 in primer, with an extra £4 10s for cellulose finish in a choice of three colours and £10 13s 6d for the fitttings.

The cab on this meat-carrying van body by W. T. Bright, also on a Chevrolet LQ, was of a style more associated with the mid-1920s, with open sides and unglazed half door. The tall build of the body was to allow carcases to be hung from rails near the top. It was also on display at Olympia in November 1931, priced at £230 in primer or £242 painted in what were described as 'ordinary' colours, including the interior in leadless white.

The Chevrolet 12-cwt model also continued, and this example with Spurling lorry bodywork was also at the 1931 Show.

four-speed gearbox having straight-cut sliding gears, quite tolerant of drivers who were often less than skilled despite its lack of synchromesh, though perhaps best remembered for its unmistakeable wailing tone, ceasing when top was engaged, when the quietness and smoothness of the engine became fully apparent. The brakes were of mechanically-operated pattern, without servo.

In terms of appearance, the most obvious difference from the Chevrolet lay in the radiator, though even this was of similar general shape and similarly finished in black stove enamel as standard. The hard-edged contours of the LQ version were replaced by a more rounded cross-section, and the radiator badge bore the Bedford name under a drawing of the mythical griffin already used on Vauxhall products and with a history going back to its choice by Fulk le Brent back in the 13th century. The words 'Made in England' also appeared in discreet yet proud lettering.

Clearly, the value, with the WHG chassis priced at £198, only £8 more than the 30-cwt LQ, and the WLG at £210, was outstanding and with the Chevrolet already familiar as an assurance to buyers who might have been

The interior of the standard cab was simple, the design being common to both the Chevrolet 30-cwt and Bedford 2-ton models. The upper part of the windscreen opened, the small windscreen wiper being mounted on its frame, and the door windows wound down. The seats were quite comfortable and it was quite easy for the driver to get out via the nearside door if preferred.

Above: 'Old No.1'. This was the very first Bedford bus, a WHB model, chassis number 100001, dating from August 1931. It had 14-seat bodywork by the Waveney Co Ltd of Oulton Broad, Lowestoft, a concern which built a number of bodies on early Bedford buses but which later concentrated on Commer chassis. This photograph shows it as running in the early 1950s with its original owner, John E. Woodham of Melchbourne. TM 9347 was still looking quite smart though only the support bracket of the front bumper remains, and there appears to be king-pin or bearing wear on the offside front wheel, which has the slight 'knock-kneed' look that was not uncommon on elderly Bedford models of this generation.

Left: The same vehicle is seen (left) after acquisition in 1961 by the Arlington Motor Co Ltd, who had supplied it, and subsequent light restoration. The front bumper fitted is thought not to be of original type. This remarkable bus has taken part in quite a number of historic commercial vehicle rallies and is one of very few cases where the first production vehicle of a whole family of models has survived. The short WHB model was never common, only 102 being built before the model was dropped in 1933.

expected to react cautiously to a new name, sales surged ahead. Complete dropside lorries with factory-built bodies cost £240 and £260 respectively. The sight, and sound, of Bedford vehicles soon became part of the landscape all over Britain.

Four months later, corresponding passenger models appeared, designated WHB and WLB, and intended for 14- and 20-seat bodywork respectively. These were closely related to the WHG and WLG respectively, with the same wheelbase figures, and thus the logic of Bedford model designations began to become clear. Yet there was no attempt to use them for publicity purposes or even in press descriptions or specification lists, the types being described simply by their weight or seating capacity classes. That

The sales of Bedford passenger models soared as soon as they were introduced, the overwhelming majority favouring the longer WLB model, as in this case. This 1932 example with Rainforth 20-seat bodywork is seen in March 1933 loading passengers in Long Eaton, Nottingham, on a local service to Draycott. Note the side lamps, mounted on each side of the windscreen rather than on the front mudguards, the plus-fours of the gentleman about to board and the cloche hats favoured by a passer-by and the conductress, the presence of the latter suggesting this was quite a busy service as driver-only operation was quite common for buses of this size.

seems to have been a matter of General Motors policy, though the letter designations act as a much clearer guide, and in later years this attitude became less marked.

The early Bedford was well suited to bus or coach duty, the different specification of the WHB and WLB including more resilient springs. A chromium-plated radiator was standard, and this was also sometimes fitted to goods models where considered preferable by the purchaser. The level of instant success may be gathered from the fact that in the last quarter of 1931, a period beginning the month after their introduction, 52% of all 14-20-seat buses and coaches registered in Britain were Bedfords.

The very first Bedford bus, a WHB with 14-seat Waveney body and having chassis number 100001, was sold on 28th August 1931 to John E. Woodham, of 15, High Street, Melchbourne, about 14 miles from Bedford, into which town, appropriately enough, he used it to run a local bus service. It soon became known locally as the Melchbourne Flyer and remained in service with Mr Woodham for 21 years. It was then used for non-PSV duties for some years before being sold and, later, acquired in 1961 by the Arlington Motor Co Ltd, who had originally

supplied it and who were among the leading Bedford coach dealers for many years.

In 1969, after restoration, my colleague Alan Townsin, then Editor of *Bus & Coach*, was invited to drive it and recalls that it would set off from rest with much the same gusto so typical of later petrol-engined Bedfords, there being the same combination of mild induction roar and the typical wailing gearbox noise. There was virtually no vibration, save for brief clutch judder as it moved off, typical of the model. As speed rose, it was clear that the performance became more restricted, breathing being limited by similar design to the LQ, with updraught carburettor, though the actual unit in this case was a Zenith U-type. Alan doesn't claim extensive experience with crash gearboxes, but found this one quite forgiving, mistimed gearchanges usually going through with no more than a slight grunt. Steering was easy if not especially precise but at the time the brakes were not performing well, apparently due to the linkage not being set up correctly, for a test report in the March 1932 Bus & Coach had praised them, with a respectable 64% Tapley reading.

In practice, not very many WHB models were built, the

Some early Bedford buses were quite austere – these two had been fitted with second-hand bodywork, with crudely-constructed windscreens to adapt them to the new chassis. They were used by Mr H. C. Simmons of Dover to carry 400 men daily to the Betteshanger, Snowdown and Tilmanstone collieries in the days when Kent had quite a busy coalfield. The far vehicle was registered KJ 4382, which was issued in late 1931. The rear overhang of the nearer vehicle is shorter than standard, another legacy of the transfer of its body from an earlier chassis. The goods-type front bumper, lack of chromium on the radiators and other fittings raises the question as to whether they might have been on the WLG chassis rather than the WLB, though certainly of the longer wheelbase version of either.

Duple soon began to become established as the likeliest choice of bodybuilder on a Bedford chassis, aided by joint marketing publicity. This 1932 WLB model, with bodywork to a pattern typical of early examples from that bodybuilder on this chassis, was operated by Bethesda Pullman Saloon on local services. This photograph, apparently dating from the mid-'thirties, is another to show the slight 'knock-kneed' look characteristic of the type after a time – the use of worn tyres was typical of the period, such being regarded as legal as long as the canvas wasn't showing, but the greater wear towards the inside edge suggests that alignment needed attention.

The coach version of Duple's standard body for the WLB as being built in 1932 generally had a hinged entrance door, curtains and an opening roof, although individual details varied. This one, registered in Brighton as UF 8619, was operated by Pownall's. Some 1,895 WLB models were built in the period of production which continued until 1935.

market for 14-seat buses, quite healthy in the 1920s, being in sharp decline as economics were tending to favour larger vehicles, and this model was dropped in 1933, but the WLB became a firm favourite in the 20-seat class, being used in both bus and coach forms. When introduced, prices of £250 for a 14-seater bus body and £265 for a 20-seater were being quoted, though in practice these were more in the nature of guide prices, Bedford operating a similar system of working with approved bodybuilders to that already in force with Chevrolet in Britain.

For the Commercial Motor Show held in November 1931, joint arrangements were made for publicising the Bedford and Chevrolet ranges, and bodybuilders with 20-seat bus bodies on Bedford chassis included Waveney, of Lowestoft, and Grose, of Northampton, both at £280 (the complete vehicles being £545), while Duple, at Hendon, quoted £550 for the complete bus. Detail design of the

bodies varied and another illustrated was Rainforth, of Lincoln, which had bodied a WLB for the Lincolnshire Road Car Co Ltd, a major user – quite possibly the largest in Britain – of the Chevrolet LQ in bus form.

Similar arrangements were in operation for the more specialised goods bodywork, and notable among these in the same 1931 Show list were Spurling, of Hendon, displaying various variations to suit the needs of farmers or market gardeners – in view of recent controversy about the transport of cattle, it is noteworthy that the then Ministry of Agriculture and Fisheries had issued an order laying down requirements for the standards to be reached in vehicle on such use some 65 years ago, though the distances then in mind were more likely to rarely exceed the distance to the nearest market. Grose was showing a van on a 30-cwt Chevrolet and W. T. Bright a tall van designed to carry carcases of meat on the same chassis.

Bedford's association with passenger transport was broader than the production of bus and coach chassis. Here a 1932 WHG tipper, GG 7424, from Glasgow Corporation Transport is seen at work. Glasgow operated one of the largest tramway systems in Britain and there would be plenty of work for tippers in track and roadway repairs. Purchase of such vehicles by municipalities was normally determined by tender, and Bedford's keen prices secured many orders, quite apart from those placed by contractors, builders etc. Tipper work is hard on rear axles, and Bedford's sturdy fully-floating design, in which the half-shafts were relieved of load-bearing stress, was well-suited to such work – this view shows the large-diameter hub quite clearly.

Another type of municipal operation in which Bedford vehicles soon became involved was refuse collection, this WLG being supplied to the cleansing department of Sowerby Bridge Urban District Council. In those days, bodies of this general type, with side-opening covers into which the dustmen tipped the bins they carried from householders' doors, were usual. Quite a high proportion of the early Bedford models were supplied without cab, this being considered as part of the bodybuilder's work and, although not unlike the standard product, this one differs in various details, appearing to be slightly broader than standard, possibly to give a little more room for two workers to be carried in addition to the driver.

It is noteworthy that both Duple and Spurling had addresses at The Hyde, Hendon, very near the General Motors premises. Duple had moved there from its original premises in Hornsey, a few miles away, in 1925, having built bus and, especially, coach bodywork on a wide variety of chassis makes and continuing to do so, though for half-a-century henceforth to be strongly associated with Bedford. Similar remarks applied on the goods side to Spurling. Clearly the proximity of these firms in a locality which was somewhat in the nature of a trading estate attracted the attention of General Motors, and obviously it would be helpful, especially in meeting a rapid order, for chassis which had come to the GM premises for testing to be bodied nearby, but the association continued long after Bedford chassis ceased being delivered via GM's Hendon premises.

Another factor which influenced this development for bus and coach bodies was the effect of the Conditions of Fitness Regulations introduced as a consequence of the Road Traffic Act 1930, some of which came into effect from 1st January 1932. They clarified dimensional requirements for entrances and gangways among other features, and the expectation was that there would be more standardisation, with a system of type approval coming into use. This proved to be only partially true, but it did encourage co-operation on designs, and the WLB with standard 20-seat body was one of the first to be given a type certificate.

Duple was not the only concern working with Bedford in this way – another concern active as a builder of approved bodywork for the model at the time was Willmotts Motors Ltd of Shepherd's Bush, again in the London area and not unduly far from Hendon. The passenger models had the fuel tank mounted on the frame side, and the WLB's 12-volt lighting, using Lucas equipment, apart from a CAV dynamo, was doubtless regarded as preferable to the 6-volt system of the Chevrolet.

The low price and good reputation of the 2-ton Bedford led to adaptations to extend its capability. Six-wheel conversions had been used on Chevrolet models and were produced for the Bedford by Baico and Spurling within the first year, as were articulated conversions of the short-chassis version by Carrimore and Scammell.

Publicity stunts were a common means of attracting attention, and in November 1931 a Bedford truck was driven for three days and nights non-stop, fuel being replenished while it was driven in that ultra-low first gear. It was organised in conjunction with Atlas of Newport, Monmouthshire (now Gwent) and despite appalling conditions and the local hilly terrain, the vehicle covered 1,268 miles.

The next development, in April 1932, was the announcement of the WS 30-cwt model and the VYC 12-cwt, this latter called simply the Light Delivery Van. These replaced the Chevrolet LQ and AC series respectively, and their relationship to those models was even more obvious than with the 2-ton model, as they had the Chevrolet-style disc wheels and semi-floating rear axle. The WS, with 131in wheelbase, had the same engine as the 2-ton model, in those days generally referred to by its RAC rating of 26.33hp although sometimes rounded up to 27hp as applied on cars so powered for taxation purposes. Prototypes of this model had been built considerably earlier, probably in 1930, followed by a batch of 31 export chassis.

The VYC, though also externally much like its Chevrolet predecessor apart from the Bedford radiator, had a smaller engine. This was the 16.9hp unit of 2.1-litre capacity, again an overhead-valve six-cylinder, as produced for the Vauxhall Cadet car introduced the previous year. The standard van, with rather angular body, cost £168, and the chassis £135. Available as an option was the 26.33hp engine, in which case the model designation became VXC, this version being favoured for newspaper delivery where good acceleration was regarded as important. As had applied with the previous Chevrolet AC model, this did not have the square-cut front bumper of heavier models of that time, and the wheels were mounted on six smaller-diameter studs instead of the eight of the bigger types. Another variant offered was the seven-seat Rural Bus, based on the 12-cwt van with side windows and seats that could be rapidly displaced to leave the floor space clear for goods, but very few seem to have been built. Another passenger type based on the 12-cwt was a Metropolitan-type taxi, but

The Bedford WS 30-cwt model was announced in April 1932, just a year after the 2-tonners appeared as the first Bedfords. It was a direct replacement for the Chevrolet LQ and resembled that model very closely in external appearance, with the same style of disc wheels, with single rear tyres and small hubs at the rear. In effect it was virtually an LQ with the Bedford pressure-lubricated engine and more-rounded radiator. This one was owned by E. F. Simmons, a Nottingham glass and china dealer who ran it to the Potteries, doubtless returning with a load composed of the products of that area surrounding Stoke-on-Trent. The name on the bonnet, 'Little Lizzy', sounds almost like an echo of the 'Tin Lizzy' nickname often applied to the Model-T Ford, though in fact that was a smaller vehicle. Note the elaborately-decorated rave boards attached to the body sides.

this seems not to have gone beyond the prototype stage.

A minor change made at the end of 1932 was an increase in capacity to the factory-built van bodies for the WS 30-cwt and WHG short 2-ton model by increasing length, width and height, though prices remained unchanged at £230 and £260 respectively.

With this line-up, Bedford had widened its appeal to a greater range of users. The most obvious competitor was Ford, mainly with the AA four-cylinder models of rather similar general appearance, though Morris-Commercial, Commer and Dodge all also offered ranges of roughly equivalent character, but the Bedford had made massive inroads into the sales not only of these but also the more expensive models of equivalent weight ratings offered by

Similarly, the VYC 12-cwt Light Delivery Van also announced in April 1932 was a replacement for the Chevrolet AC van, though in this case it had the 2.1-litre Vauxhall Cadet engine by then in production. This early example had the Chev-style disc wheels with small projecting hubs used on the first year's production.

The Rural Bus version of the VYC was a rare 7-seat conversion of the standard 12-cwt van. This 1932 example was owned by R. Finch & Son, of Princetown, Devon, and brought children into Princetown School, near Dartmoor Prison, in the mornings, was used as a delivery van during the day and then took the children home at the end of the day.

Sometimes Bedford chassis received unusual types of bodywork, such as this narrow van body with no cab doors, evidently on a WS chassis. The registration number, VT 8092, indicates issue in Stoke-on-Trent in 1932, but the photograph, thought to date from the late 1930s, shows the kind of deterioration some vehicles suffered – sadly, Bedfords, inexpensive when new and depreciating sharply if fitted with bodywork judged to be outdated in later years, as doubtless applied here, were quite prone to such neglect despite their good durability.

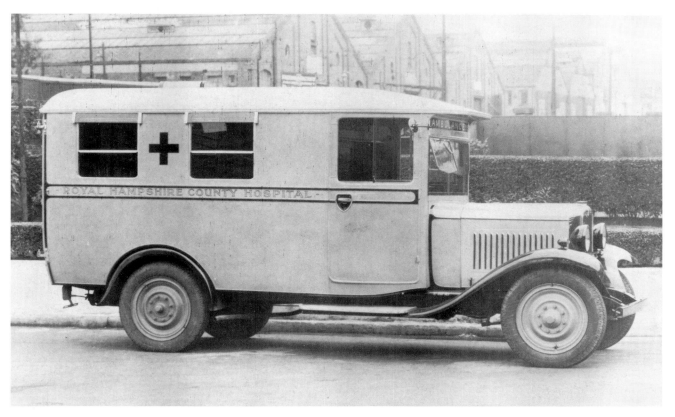

With its smooth, quiet six-cylinder engine, the WS model was basically well suited to ambulance work and over the years many examples of this and subsequent 30-cwt types were sold for such duty – at a later stage, ambulance versions of the chassis were offered as a regular option, with softer springing and other detail changes to the specification. This one dating from 1932 for the Royal Hampshire County Hospital had a body of high-waisted style typical of the period. Note the chromium-plated radiator, as often specified for such vehicles.

firms like Dennis, Guy, Leyland and Thornycroft.

Bedford was also competing in the export market, and while this would doubtless have been co-ordinated by General Motors headquarters to some degree, Bedford did not simply collect business from Empire markets where British products and right-hand steering were favoured, though there were many such cases. Rather remarkably, 88 2-tonners were shipped to the Soviet Union in June 1932, for example. By the end of that year 12,000 Bedfords had been sold, and 65% of all buses and coaches in the 9-20-seat class first registered in Britain in 1932 were Bedfords.

Another development that year was the introduction, in June, of the Bedford Transport Magazine, succeeding earlier publications which had covered Chevrolet and, for a time, both marques, though the new magazine was produced directly by Vauxhall staff – it was to remain in production until July 1977, apart from a break during the 1939-45 war.

Developments in the earlier part of 1933 concerned

There were no clear-cut rules as to overloading in the 1930s and instances were common, though this one was probably illusory – the WLG, seemingly quite an early one, judging by the style of cab, seems not to have been riding any lower on its springs than was to be expected. Apart from the general unwieldy nature of the load, need for care when cornering, in negotiating low bridges and overhanging tree branches, the main reason of concern might well have been the effect on the boat of having much of its weight carried at one point near the mid-point of its length. It appears to have been a ship's lifeboat, doubtless being carried for conversion to some other function.

The Bedford 8-cwt van, type ASYC or ASXC, introduced in June 1933, was a close derivative of the Vauxhall Light Six car which first appeared the previous month. The standard van body incorporated the front doors and windscreen assembly of the equivalent Vauxhall saloon and the chassis, including items such as wheels and mudguards, was virtually identical apart from the lack of the Vauxhall flutes on the radiator and bonnet top. Such a vehicle looked smart and up-to-date, as well as having quite lively performance, even with the 12hp engine, appealing to an enterprising business that wanted to look 'different', as no doubt applied to A. Bailey & Son, running Keston Farm Dairy of South Norwood – the registration, OY 6624, was issued in Croydon around the late summer of 1933, very possibly being taken out by the dealer selling the van, as was common practice. Note the 'Non Combine' lettering, an indication of the dominance of the large dairy groups even at that time.

**The Vauxhall Light Six, in this case a drop-head.**

vans. In May the VYC and VXC changed to wire wheels with chromium-plated hub caps of the style then being used on Vauxhall cars. A more important event was the announcement in June of a new 8-cwt van, based on the Vauxhall Light Six car model which had appeared in May, and represented a major shift in policy towards the manufacture of smaller-engined models. This was in line with the realisation at General Motors board level that it had become essential to bring Vauxhall into a higher volume category and improve its profitability – over the previous two years, the factory had built more Bedford commercial vehicles than Vauxhall cars. There were two

models, the ASY 12hp of 1,503cc and the ASX 14hp of 1,781cc, both six-cylinder in what had become a Vauxhall/Bedford tradition and in line with quite widespread interest in relatively small-capacity six-cylinder cars in Britain at that time. Some of these proved to be unsatisfactory, with unreliable engines barely more refined than four-cylinder units but this was not so of the Vauxhalls, possibly the most successful of the lower-priced examples at the time.

In many respects, with their smooth and quiet-running engines, they could be regarded as a scaled-down interpretation of the Chevrolet policy, and the Bedford versions, ASYC and ASXC, the latter relatively uncommon, brought new standards of refinement to the smaller delivery van. The 12hp was the cheapest six-cylinder goods model on the market, offering remarkable value at £155 complete. Clearly it gained from, and helped to swell, the volume of production which made this possible, the mechanical design being common to car and van versions. The common design features were very obvious in terms of appearance, extending to the swept

Another early AS-series van, in this case registered JH 5813 for the St Albans Co-operative Society butchery department. These photographs with staff rather obviously posed were doubtless taken for the publicity department.

The larger WS continued with its more conservative lines. The reverse of this photograph of one dating from 1933 is inscribed 'police ambulance', though the appearance might suggest that it was a 'Black Maria', for the transport of miscreants. The functions of the various organisations were sometimes less clear cut than in later times, especially in the smaller towns, as perhaps also indicated by the fact that the picture was posed in front of the fire station. Tynemouth, on the whole a very 'respectable' place in those days, seems rather unlikely to have needed a Black Maria. Note the bulb horn, an outdated feature doubtless specified by the police, apt to be conservative in such things. The standard Bedford horn of the time was of the Klaxon type, with its unmistakeable 'a-oo-er' sound – it was made by another General Motors subsidiary.

Another 8-cwt AS-type dairy van. In this case a body with open sides having shutters was required and the vehicle was evidently supplied in 'chassis-scuttle' form, having only the windscreen assembly of the standard body, upon which a bodybuilder produced a complete body to suit the customer's needs. Sproston's Dairy was in Nantwich, Cheshire, the vehicle being registered AMB 286 in that county.

mudguards and the front part of the standard van body, save that the radiator and bonnet did not have the fluting at the top corners which was a Vauxhall feature of those days.

Synchromesh, making gear-changing easier by adding small cone clutches within the gearbox to bring relative gear speeds to conformity before engagement was made, had been a General Motors development, first offered on Cadillac models in 1928. It was first offered by Vauxhall on the Cadet model in 1931, and the 8-cwt van had this feature on third and top gears from new, a good selling point when delivery vans were liable to be in the hands of inexperienced drivers. The model remained in production until 1939, outliving the car version, superseded after 1934 – this continued production of van versions of models for longer than the related Vauxhall car, occurred on other occasions during the Bedford story.

Bedford sales reached 16,000 during 1933, that year's production thus easily exceeding those of 1931 and 1932 together.

The idea of a dual-purpose vehicle, capable of carrying passengers or goods probably has its roots in the horse-drawn country carrier's cart of Victorian or even earlier times, and versions based on motor vehicles were fairly common up to the mid-1920s but had almost died out by the 1930s. This vehicle operated by W. V. Roberts of Petworth, Sussex was based on a Bedford WLB chassis, with what appears to be Duple bus bodywork of the style standard at the time. It had a special removable rear panel, itself incorporating the normal hinged emergency exit door, to allow use as a van. The panel was quite heavy, and in the view above Mr Roberts and his fitter take the weight while the young girl in a period gingham dress gives the photographer a slightly impish smile.

Below, MV 6093 is in use as a van, with a tailboard restrained by chains into which a crate is being lifted – the stencilling, upside down in the picture, indicates that it may have contained 'Three Musketeers' safety matches. Some of the seats have been removed and an external board fitted over the side windows. The presence of the Bedford emblem on the side suggests that the vehicle might have begun life as a demonstrator, the Middlesex registration possibly supporting that view, though the Hendon premises of both GM and Duple – the latter firm's name coming from the fact that it had specialised in smaller dual-purpose bodywork at first – had London postal district addresses. Note the unusual brickwork of the building.

Some WLB models had very active lives. This one was first registered in Perthshire in the latter part of 1932, but later passed to James Marwick of Evie, in the Orkney islands, and by 1946, when this picturesque scene was photographed, had covered 300,000 miles. It was used on a service connecting Evie and Fursin which operated on three days a week, intended for local inhabitants rather than tourists, though legally the latter could not have been refused on a licensed stage carriage service. In this case the roof was fixed and slatted, allowing it to carry items that would not fit within – the shape of the securing rail suggests that it had been used in this way. Vehicles of this size and character were almost ideally suited to operation in remote places. Had the soldier just returned from the war, one wonders?

The style of interior of a typical Duple-bodied WLB model is well conveyed in this photograph, taken within the superbly-restored 1932 example shown below. The entrance door was of the external-opening hinged type, which implies that it was used on coach duties, but in this case the style of seat was not far removed from the bus standard of the time, and many very similar vehicles were to be found on bus work in rural areas all over Britain, but generally with folding doors at that date. Note how the driver sat quite near the centre-line of the vehicle, a legacy of the car-related origins of the original design – it was necessary to stretch the right arm to the full to make a signal visible to drivers of following vehicles, and no direction indicators of any type were provided in those days. A sliding roof was fitted, again rather a 'coach' feature though sometimes found on buses, especially if intended for intermittent use on excursion work.

This is the exterior of the same vehicle, GV 1173, operated by F. Cross of Bury St Edmunds, Suffolk. In this case, the emergency exit door was at the offside rear, causing the rear window to be of the single-panel and giving a more 'coach'-like rear view.

# 5 THE WT – A NEW GENERATION BEGINS

Stepney Acre's masterpiece – the 30mph 3-tonner in its original form as introduced at the Commercial Motor Show of November 1933, the example shown being the WTL long-wheelbase version, with a standard dropside body. The model introduced a completely new and purposeful look to medium-sized commercial vehicles, setting a pattern to be followed, save for various styling changes, by succeeding Bedford types until the 1950s, and copied in varying ways by many other makers. Its basis was far more than cosmetic, being one of logical use of space and sensible weight distribution. The radiator design was, in general appearance, very like those on other Bedford models, at first retaining the exposed honeycomb core, but given a different look in its new position – this example had a chromium-plated shell, found only on a minority of this model, though available to order. This illustration had been retouched for use in a catalogue and it seems that the artist had slightly misunderstood the shape of the front wing, just behind the bumper, in applying a highlight.

At the Commercial Motor Show of November 1933, the main exhibit on the Bedford stand, a new 3-ton model, the WT, created a sensation. Searching for a phase to sum it up, the trade press referred to it as the '30mph 3-tonner', because up to that date it had generally been considered that a vehicle capable of carrying 3 tons would inevitably weigh more than 2 tons 10 cwt unladen, and hence be limited in its legal maximum speed to 20mph under contemporary legislation.

The only commercial vehicles allowed to travel at 30mph were goods models below that unladen weight limit, or buses and coaches. These speed limits applied anywhere and hence the effect on journey times was considerable, so a good deal of general haulage, especially of commodities where rapid delivery was important, was carried on lorries such as the Bedford 2-ton models. The WT not only met the weight requirement with a standard dropside body, but was advertised as 'the truck for the 50% overload' in those more casual days on such matters, widening its appeal even further.

The WT set new standards in more than meeting the 2 tons 10 cwt unladen weight limit, which also kept the annual road tax down to £30 at that time. It was designed by P. Stepney Acres, and the ideas he incorporated influenced almost all manufacturers of goods vehicles in this weight category over the next 20 years or so. It was of what became known as semi-forward-control layout – journalists describing it at the time were clearly struggling to find suitable words in more ways than one. The idea of forward control, with driver alongside the engine, was well established by then, though more usually found on commercial vehicles in heavier categories. The phrase 'normal control' referred to the car-like arrangement, with the driving position behind the engine. Semi-forward control was thus a half-way house between the two.

However, another key factor in the whole front-end layout of the vehicle was the position of the engine and radiator in relation to the front axle. Until around 1930, it was usual, on both sides of the Atlantic, for cars to have the radiator set directly over the front axle. A more forward-set radiator was common on heavier commercial vehicles, going right back to Edwardian times. Oddly enough, among the very few instances of this among cars of that period were some Napier models with very large six-cylinder engines – could it be that Stepney Acres had been influenced by them when he worked for that firm, prior to 1927, for this formed part of his new design?

The early Bedfords, with their roots in American car

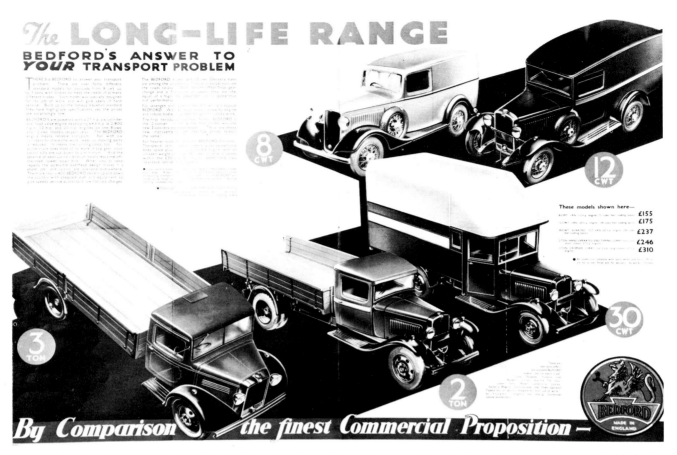

This 1934 brochure illustrates how the WT made the rest of Bedford's models, save perhaps for the small 8-cwt van, look quite dated even though they were to remain in production at least until late in 1936. The models shown are a 3-ton WTL with dropside body, priced at £310; a 2-ton WHG hand-operated tipper, £246; a 30-cwt boarded tilt van, £237; a 12-cwt van, by then of the 20hp BYC type, £175, and an 8-cwt 12hp ASYC van, £155. It is noteworthy that the engine of the larger models is referred to as the 27hp unit, despite the actual RAC rating of 26.66hp, the rounding-up was logical in the sense that this was how the taxation rates were applied.

practice as it had stood in 1929, belonged to the 'radiator over the axle' school, but by 1933 there was a clear trend for radiators on cars and light commercials to be moved further forward and the set-back radiator was just beginning to look a little old-fashioned.

The WT was itself quite influential in causing this to become even more strongly evident among commercial vehicles by about 1935, though its design may well have come about by straightforward analysis of the more efficient use of space and better weight distribution. On models such as the earlier Bedfords, especially in short-wheelbase form, the weight of the load was carried almost entirely by the rear axle, and the space available to carry it was barely half the length of the vehicle.

By moving the radiator and engine forward, more space for the load (or, on a bus, passengers) was released. Full forward control would have given more still, but this would have involved more complex design and, for a medium-sized vehicle, there would probably have been some customer resistance. By simply moving the driving position forward so that the toe-board of the cab was part-way alongside the engine, valuable space was gained without mechanical complexity. Indeed the combination of these two features gave a space saving directly comparable to some particularly ungainly-looking versions of full

forward-control of about that time, where the radiator was not moved forward. Some of these were conversions, among them some based on the early Bedford models.

The WT series Bedford was designed with subtle artistry – to the casual glance, it simply seemed to have a very short bonnet. By tapering the bonnet sides sharply outwards from the radiator, they met the cab at the windscreen pillars and the projection forward of the part of the cab accommodating the driver's and passenger's feet was accommodated under this wider part of the bonnet.

This arrangement meant that the driver's controls were quite normal, save that the gear lever was inclined forwards slightly, and this was not enough to make its movements awkward – in fact it was probably slightly beneficial in this respect, producing an almost upright lever, giving a comfortable action. The driver sat slightly higher than on the WLG, etc, and forward vision over the short bonnet was good. It was possible for drivers to exit from the nearside of the cab if need be, even if getting one's feet round the engine cowl was slightly awkward. Removable panels allowed access to the rear portion of the engine from within the cab.

There were two versions of the model. The WTH, with 111in (9ft 3in) wheelbase very soon became a great favourite with tipper operators not only because its compact size

A demand for longer bodywork had already caused some operators to have forward-control conversions of WLG models as well as other makes, involving quite extensive, and expensive, modifications to move the steering box forward to a point where it was exposed ahead of the radiator, altering the position of the pedals and the construction of a special cab with internal engine cover. The end-result, while gaining an extra 2ft or so of useful body length, was apt to be ungainly-looking and offered awkward access to driver and passenger as well as to the engine. This example for B. Hopewell of Mansfield, dating from about 1933 had a cab and body by Duple, and even that firm's designers' usually good eyes for appearance had clearly found the job difficult. The normal front wings and running board were retained, the latter mostly under the front end of the body. Note how the operator's routes covered several industrial cities and ports.

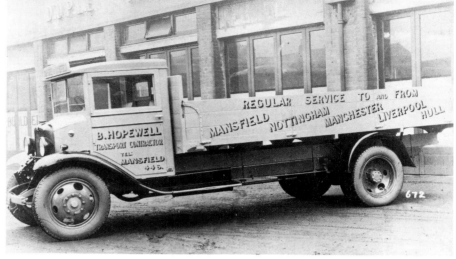

Another interpretation of the same idea, operated by Southampton Corporation Waterworks, where clearly the means to transport long lengths of pipe were essential. This 1933 WLG, OW 3393, had a different style of cab, with a flat panel immediately behind the radiator swept round to merge with the sides and having a step effect in front of the windscreen. Overall it was perhaps a little tidier, but the set-back radiator and swept wing-line did not blend well with a style better suited to a chassis with radiator further forward.

The WTL, with the same wheelbase as the WLG, but with the engine and radiator moved forward and semi-forward-control, offered similar body length to the above conversions while retaining most of the simplicity associated with the bonneted layout, and a more harmonious appearance as a bonus. Note the hinged cab roof ventilator on this 1934 example – a simple device but quite effective in its purpose, and desirable in a WT model on a warm day, as the engine cowl did convey rather more heat into the cab than on a true normal-control model, welcome in winter but needing effective ventilation in summer. This was an early production example, used for press road tests in August 1934.

made it very manoeuvrable in tight spaces but also because the compact front-end reduced the stresses in the frame which were a source of trouble with vehicles of the old-style normal-control layout working over rough ground. The WTL had the same wheelbase as the WLG, 157in (13ft 1in), but the change in design allowed the body to have a clear length within of 14ft. The weight distribution put a little more weight on the front axle and the steering was lower geared to compensate for this, needing 4½ turns from lock to lock instead of 2¼ for the WLG.

The engine was basically the same 26.33hp, but the design was revised, with better breathing via a downdraught Zenith carburettor, and gave 64bhp at 2,800rpm. It still had cast-iron pistons, but these were of a concave crown type, intended to improve the shape of the combustion chamber, a subject in which Vauxhall, and General Motors, took great interest.

The brakes were given a vacuum servo, though the operation at that stage was mechanical, by means of cables – The Commercial Motor, in its report on a WTL in August

The short-wheelbase WTH soon became a very familiar sight as a tipper, major contractors such as Wimpey's rapidly building up big fleets. Continuous work on uneven ground puts severe stress on the frames of tippers and the stubby build of this model proved itself to be particularly suited to such conditions. The vehicle nearer the camera on the right has the vertically slatted radiator grille introduced in the latter part of 1935, but the design of this model was otherwise unchanged.

Part of the secret of the compact front end of the WT models was the way in which part of the engine was housed under the dashboard of the cab. This view shows the effect when opening the bonnet – in effect, only the front three cylinders of the six extended beyond the boxes housing the pedals and driver's and passenger's feet. This did mean that access to the sparking plugs of the rear three cylinders was not quite so easy as on previous models, though still possible, and removable covers within the cab provided for more major work.

1934, reported that the brake pedal required no more pressure than the clutch pedal and speculated as to whether the degree of assistance had been overdone. Fuel consumption, with a 3-ton payload and a gross weight of 5 tons 12 cwt 2 qr, worked out at 12.6mpg. The complete vehicle with dropside body cost £310, and the chassis with standard cab – Bedford models were often sold in this form – was £285, the shorter WTH being £270.

A modest face-lift was carried out to the 8-cwt 'Light Six' ASYC and ASXC van with effect from December 1933, when larger hub caps, front mudguards that swept lower at the front and dual windscreen wipers became standard.

The WTL and WTH went into production in the Spring of 1934, and soon Bedford began to use the slogan "You see them everywhere" for its extended range of models – brilliantly simple and having the merit of being true. The economics of new vehicles of low first cost, relatively cheap to run, generally very reliable and yet simple to repair when the need arose made many operators abandon their previous policy of running older vehicles. At that time, there were still many of the war-surplus models

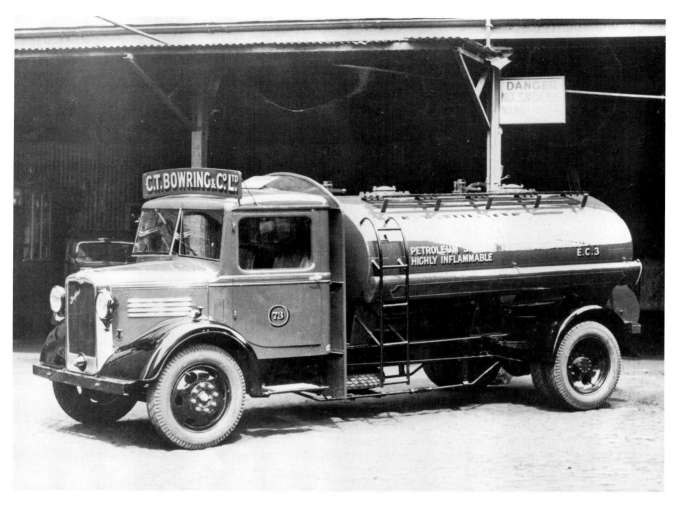

The WTL looked well when smartly painted, having that characteristic of visually harmonious designs of accepting almost any livery, though in the case of this petrol tanker owned by C. T. Bowring & Co Ltd of London E.C.3 there were clear indications of pride in appearance in the choice of chromium-plated radiator and discreet lining-out. Note the full-depth guard behind the cab needed to comply with petroleum regulations. Bowring was representative of the smaller petrol distribution companies active in the pre-war and earlier post-war era – the WTL was also favoured by the big-name companies, several of which ran large fleets of the type and its O-type successors.

From December 1933, the 8-cwt ASYC van received similar minor changes in its appearance as were applied to the corresponding 1934 model of the Vauxhall Light Six car – front mudguards that swept down further at the front and larger hub caps. These were in line with general styling trends at the time, and in addition the model received dual windscreen wipers as standard, instead of the single one sweeping only an area directly in front of the driver as had been the standard previously.

The model was to remain in production in this form until 1939, by which date the equivalent car had been through two changes of style and the wire wheels of the van had become quite a dated feature, as they had gone out of fashion, except for cars of sporting character, in which case they would have the knock-off eared type of hub nut. This example of the model was supplied to a dairy on the island of Jersey, hence the registration number with single-letter J mark. It appeared that milk was still being supplied by jug rather than bottle, a system still occasionally found on the mainland at about that date.

The VYC 12-cwt delivery van also received the larger chromium-plated hub caps for the 1934 season, as shown by the example on the left in this view, thought to show vehicles belonging to the Burnley police – on the right is a WS 30-cwt, understood to have been an ambulance. The view shows how the VYC had a lower build, largely due to the smaller diameter wheels, at this stage. The VYC carries a Bedford Driver's Club badge below the offside headlamp. The registration numbers, HG 2 and HG 9, are noteworthy, as the HG series had begun in 1930 and, by 1934, normal issues were well into the 2000-odd range, so it appears that this was a case of numbers specially reserved, and possibly transferred from earlier vehicles. In today's world, the numbers and the old-style petrol pump would be highly prized.

of various makes that could be bought quite cheaply after the 1914-18 war on the road. They had given good service but were comparatively slow, quite apart from being subject to the 20mph legal limit because of their weight, but increasingly they were being pensioned-off in favour of new fleets of lighter models, and Bedfords in particular.

Also established that year was the Bedford Drivers' Club, which, among other things, offered free insurance to drivers and produced a list of approved eating places – it was to continue until 1968 and many Bedfords carried the blue BDC badge, based on a steering wheel emblem.

The 30-cwt and 2-ton models continued unaltered in appearance, contrasting oddly with the new 3-tonners, but in June 1934 the torque-tube drive was dropped in favour of a conventional open propellor shaft and what was called the 'tipped' rear axle casing, with the joint face inclined,

standard from the beginning on the WT. The idea behind this was to minimise the depth of the casing, so improving ground clearance, of value when negotiating rough ground.

It was hardly surprising that bus and coach operators expressed interest in the WT series of models. The WLB, much as introduced in 1931, remained as the listed model in this category until the Autumn of 1935 and continued to sell, in smaller numbers than earlier, but in histories of the marque it is apt to be forgotten that a passenger adaptation of the WTL was introduced at the Scottish Show in November 1934, a full year before a the fully redesigned WTB in this category appeared.

The 26-seat version of the WTL had a 12-volt instead of 6-volt electrical system but this time there was no need to move the fuel tank, already on the frame side. The radiator was generally chromium-plated, as opposed to the

The occasional instance of a Vauxhall with a 'commercial' type of body arose, as in the case of this Big Six model with what would nowadays be called a pick-up body, though the term was unknown in Britain at the time. The body was built to special order by Duple around the early months of 1935. The Big Six was produced in two models, the 20hp BY, and the BX, with basically the same 26.33hp unit as the larger Bedfords, this latter being marketed as the 27hp. It appeared at the end of 1933 and was closely resembled by a new generation of Light Six models a year later, but the Big Six, apart from being larger, was readily identifiable by the streamlined sidelights. The body seems likely to have been built for a private buyer, possibly for use on a large estate, and is posed in the forecourt of the bodybuilder's premises in Hendon – note the time exposure image of passing traffic, possibly a tram, shortly before the conversion of the route along the Edgware Road to trolleybuses.

Although the WLB remained Bedford's passenger model as listed in reference lists until November 1935, the potential of the WTL for passenger work soon caught bodybuilders' and operators' attention, and bowing to this demand, a passenger version of the model was introduced for the 1935 season. A high proportion of Bedford buses and coaches sold in 1935 were of this type. A typical example was No.39, registered AWR 97 and thought to date from about January of that year, in the fleet of Ezra Laycock, of Barnoldswick, in the West Riding of Yorkshire, one of the oldest established independent bus operators in the country.

It had a 26-seat Duple bus body of a style quite common on this chassis, having general appearance quite similar to earlier types as built on WLB models, though the rather fussy-looking detail treatment of the destination box, easily mistaken as a design from an earlier period, was a recent innovation. This example had the emergency door at the offside front and a single window at the rear, the entrance evidently being at the front, though rear-entrance bodies were not uncommon on 1935 WTL or WLB chassis. Although the chromium radiator was fitted, the passenger WTL models generally conformed to the goods vehicle specification in the style of front bumper and lack of cover over the front wheel nuts.

As a basis of comparison, a broadly similar design of Duple body, with the same destination box design, is seen on a WLB supplied to Bethesda Pullman Saloon around mid-1935. The overall appearance of JC 2846 had changed very little from that of the 1932 example, JC 747, for the same fleet shown on page 34. As with many Bedfords of this era, the characteristic diamond tread pattern of Goodyear tyres is evident.

Another WTL with Duple bus-outline body, in this case with rear emergency exit but more coach-like seats and a sliding roof. It dated from mid-1935 but was photographed in March 1938. It was operated by Elliott Bros, of Ben Lomond Garage, Jamestown, using the fleetname 'Pioneer', being registered SN 6850 by Dumbarton County Council. Note the varying expressions of the occupants caught by the photographer. Another identifying feature of the WTL is in the chassis number range, in the 874xxx to early 876xxx series for most passenger examples. as opposed to the series from 110001 used for the somewhat similar but slightly later WTB.

Willowbrook was a bodybuilder which, in the mid- to late-1930s, tended to specialise in quite stylish bodywork which was suited to both bus and coach duties. This WTL, JU 6301, was placed in service in mid-1935 by 'Brown's Blue', L. D. Brown, of Markfield, Leicestershire, A cleaner appearance was given by the smooth profile with matching destination and illuminated fleet-name display panels. There was a sliding roof – this passing under a roof-mounted luggage rack – and the seats were of a comfortable-looking style, yet the door was of the folding type then generally favoured for bus work.

By no means all of Duple's bodies on the WTL chassis were utilitarian in appearance. This one, for Greenslade's Tours, of Exeter, apparently registered AFJ 782 and thus seemingly dating from the summer of 1935, from what can be seen of the registration plate, has clear hints of later ideas in its styling. At that time, the type of coach with fully-opening roof was still strongly in favour in Devon, and although the position in which this picture was posed does not make it obvious at first glance, the hood is down in this view, being visible, folded, at the rear. The wide window bays were doubtless to help passengers have a good view of Dartmoor scenery, and the falling cantrail line towards the front gives a hint of later Vista designs, though the overall effect is rather nearer the Hendonian body of the later 1930s. The front mudguard shape, doubtless a high-grade welding job based on the standard product, as was quite common practice in those days, almost echoes the WLB shape, though modernised with a deep valance. The very wide emergency door must have created structural problems, especially in a body lacking the rigidity of a solid roof structre. In this case, a chromium front bumper has been added, its exaggerated forward sweep suggesting nervousness about the WTL's forward-mounted radiator.

There had always been a good deal of cross-over between the use to which goods and passenger Bedford models were put. Cases of WLG chassis with passenger bodies were quite commonplace, some thought to go back to the earlier months of 1931, before the WLB passenger equivalent became available. An instance of the reverse was the case of London Transport, which acquired a very mixed fleet of small buses from various independent operators whose businesses were compulsorily acquired under the powers it was given on formation in July 1933. Among these were over 20 Bedford buses, mainly WLB, taken over in the following year or two (mainly from operators on the fringes of its area) and numbered in a BD series, but most of the acquired small buses soon became surplus as a new fleet of oil-engined Leyland Cub buses entered service. Even so, there seems to have been some regard for the qualities of the Bedford, for several WLB buses were sent to Duple and fitted with new van bodies in 1935. Among them was AKK 458, a 20-seat bus new in 1933 and acquired with the business of Gravesend & District Bus Services Ltd in October of that year. It became BD 4, running as a bus for two years but was rebodied as shown in December 1935, retaining the same fleet number. In 1939, it became 148B in London Transport's service vehicle series and was sold in September 1946. Quite a neat van resulted, built to London Transport requirements, the WLB front bumper and hub covers being retained. In later years many Bedford goods models were bought new by London Transport.

black enamel normal for the goods version, but as on all Bedford's heavier-duty models of the time, there was no stone-guard, the honeycomb core being exposed. The 13ft 1in wheelbase was unaltered on this interim model, and the overall length of the chassis was 19ft 2³/₁₆in but with body this would have become about 21ft. A seating plan of a Duple body reproduced with a *Bus & Coach* report on the model in the issue of March 1935 showed a single sideways-facing seat over the offside rear wheel arch and five across the rear to give the 26-seat capacity; seat spacing on the right-hand side was quite tight at 2ft 3in spacing, and some users settled for a 24-seat version, but even at that the increased capacity over the WLB broadened the appeal of the model usefully and sizeable numbers of the WTL in passenger form entered service during 1935. Duple's price for a complete 26-seat coach on the WTL in March of that year was £727.

The WTB appeared as part of a revised range introduced just before the November 1935 Commercial Motor Show. It had a 167in (13ft 11in) wheelbase, and the extra 10in made possible the provision of coach bodywork with up to 26 comfortable seats for the passengers, all facing forward. Particular attention was given to the suspension – another subject on which General Motors took an interest as a matter of group policy. Although the WTB was quite orthodox in principle (unlike the Vauxhall Light Six cars, which had adopted independent front suspension in a general redesign a year earlier), the careful design of long leaf springs, of progressive action at the rear, and adoption of low-pressure 7.50-20 tyres gave the model a standard of ride better than many more expensive coaches.

A combined marketing operation was laid on with Duple, with colour brochures giving details of the range of standard bodies for the WTB by this bodybuilder. The chassis price was a remarkable £290, and with the original version of the Duple Vista body, as introduced for 1937, having 25 seats, opening roof, full-drop winding windows

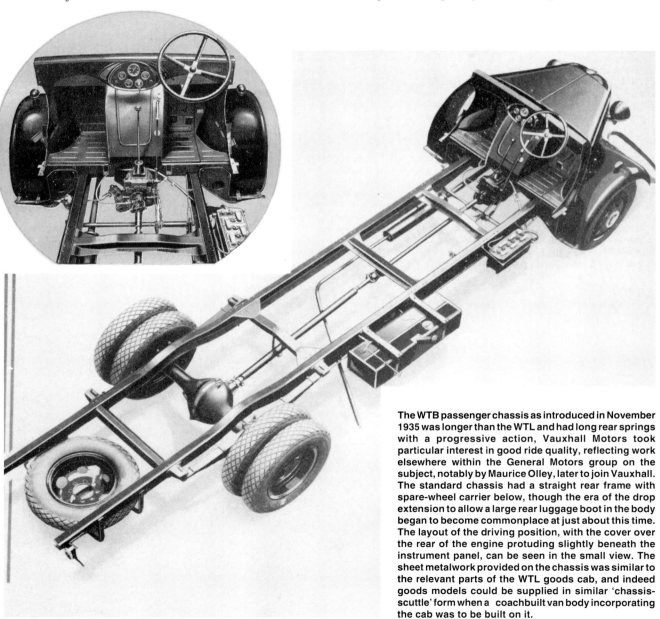

The WTB passenger chassis as introduced in November 1935 was longer than the WTL and had long rear springs with a progressive action, Vauxhall Motors took particular interest in good ride quality, reflecting work elsewhere within the General Motors group on the subject, notably by Maurice Olley, later to join Vauxhall. The standard chassis had a straight rear frame with spare-wheel carrier below, though the era of the drop extension to allow a large rear luggage boot in the body began to become commonplace at just about this time. The layout of the driving position, with the cover over the rear of the engine protuding slightly beneath the instrument panel, can be seen in the small view. The sheet metalwork provided on the chassis was similar to the relevant parts of the WTL goods cab, and indeed goods models could be supplied in similar 'chassis-scuttle' form when a coachbuilt van body incorporating the cab was to be built on it.

The key recognition point of the WTB on its introduction, distinguishing it from the stop-gap passenger version of the WTL produced in 1935, was the vertically slatted radiator grille. This also became standard on the goods range (though usually with painted shell) at the same time, including the WTL model, but the need to build passenger bodywork on the latter had vanished. Seen here on road test, very possibly for Modern Transport, which claimed its report of 4th January 1936 was the first to be published, is one of the first WTB chassis, with Duple body built to the specification of Keith & Boyle (London) Ltd, proprietors of the substantial London-based Orange Luxury Coaches fleet. Bedford Transport Magazine also reported on the test, carried out by Richard Twelvetrees, well-known technical journalist of the day, visible on the left in the peaked cap he habitually wore. The location is thought to be Succombs Hill in Surrey, a three-quarter-mile climb from Caterham Valley to Warlingham Heights regularly used by Modern Transport, the coach being posed just after the steepest section, with a gradient of 1 in 4¼, which was climbed easily in first gear with a load equivalent to 22 passengers with luggage. Estimated top speed was 50mph and 0-30mph through the gears was achieved in 19.2 seconds, which would still have been regarded as very lively for a laden coach 40 years later. Note the unusual offside mounting of the spare wheel, giving an odd appearance and requiring an almost impossible lift into position for the driver unless aid could be obtained.

This rear view of the same coach shows the folding roof and the rear boot supported by a low-level extension to the frame, rather similar to the support for the platform on a rear-entrance double-deck bus. This was the subject of patents taken out by the Keith & Boyle concern. Another feature was the ramped floor, reducing wheel-arch intrusion for passengers seated over the rear axle and also giving a better view for those in seats towards the rear of the coach. The body was known as the K. D. Special and during the 1936 season was offered for general sale in addition to being built for the Orange Luxury fleet, although the external spare wheel feature was not adopted for production versions.

The nearside view of the WTB with Duple K. D. Special body for Orange Luxury Coaches seen on the previous page shows its general lines to advantage. Whilst to the operator's specification, details of the actual styling were clearly the work of Duple's very competent draughtsmen, and most features were to be found, together or separately, on various other coaches being built around that time. The sloping-pillar feature had become quite fashionable on coaches built by various British builders over the previous year or two, and the stepped waistline was another feature in vogue for a time. In some cases, it lined up with a stepped seating level but here the level of the seats rose gently towards the rear, a revival of an idea found on some very early charabanc designs of 30 years earlier though now in much milder form. The sweeping treatment given to the rear wing was another widely-used feature, to remain a Duple characteristic until the early 1950s. Note the Royal coat of arms – discreet 'By Appointment' wording appears beneath. Someone has forgotten to fit the nearside chromium front hub cap standard on the WTB but the chromium front bumpers are evident. Among other users of the K. D. design was the Scottish Motor Traction Co Ltd, which placed 20 in service with 20-seat capacity for touring duties in 1936, numbered C46-65 in a series of which the earlier numbers were mainly WLB but included twelve Chevrolet and a GMC. A further 20 K. D. coaches, again with 20 seats, went to W. Alexander & Sons Ltd, of Falkirk, another prominent member of the SMT group.

and sliding entrance door the price complete was £825 – it was available as a 20-seater for £10 less.

These prices were less than even the chassis of a typical full-sized coach of the day, such as a Leyland Tiger, and although the latter would, typically, carry a 32-seat body, the low cost of the Bedford appealed very strongly to the typical independent operator. A Duple service bus was also offered – the late 1935 price for this as a 20-seater was £625, but far more of the coach versions were sold, and it is significant that by 1937 the leaflet for the WTB quoted details and prices of both the Vista and the slightly cheaper Hendonian coach bodies but service bus bodies were listed as being "built to order – prices on application". Duple was by far the most popular choice but other bodybuilders produced coach bodies on the WTB, such as Burlingham, Willowbrook, Willmott, Mulliner, Thurgood and many more.

It became common practice for operators of rural bus routes to use a Bedford coach for the service during the week and for excursions or private hire at week-ends, this flexibility becoming part of the economics of running such a business, often based in a village or country town. Yet Bedfords were also to be found in many city-based coach fleets and even secured a foothold among some of the major companies, such as the SMT group in Scotland, of which the parent company also acted as one of Bedford's main dealers, as well as a few municipalities – Bournemouth Corporation adopting the WTB for its sea-front service, for example. It was soon taking 55% of the British coach market, and Bedford's dominance of such business was to continue for virtually half a century.

The October 1935 changes to the range included the general adoption of the radiator grille with fine vertical slats as used on the WTB, and acting as the simplest visual distinction of this type from the passenger version of the WTL, though the greater wheelbase length was also fairly obvious. It continued to be painted as standard, except for the WTB, but could be chromium plated to order, as often favoured for such vehicles as ambulances or fire engines.

However, a more fundamental change was made in the appearance of the 30-cwt WS and the 2-ton WHG and WLG, for these all now became more akin to the WT range. Aside from more up-to-date looks, better weight distribution was claimed, and length was slightly reduced without loss of body space. The engines and radiators were moved forward and the style of mudguards and cabs also became

The WHG and WLG 2-ton models, unaltered except in small details from their introduction in 1931, had soldiered on, along with the WS 30-cwt of a year later, until late 1935, by then looking quite dated not only in comparison to the WTL but in relation to styling trends on cars and commercial vehicles generally. This WHG van belonging to a gas company, evidently in Darlington, judging by the BHN registration mark, dated from about the late summer of 1935, so would have been among the last of the type. Gas cookers were quite heavy in those days, tending to be made largely from iron castings – one suspects these two men were wishing the photographer would get the picture taken without delay – so no doubt the 2-ton van was considered more appropriate than the 30-cwt, on which this style of body, again very '1931', was more usual. Note the Bedfords Driver's Club badge in its usual place on the bumper and the muff covering the lower part of the radiator – the starting handle may well have been useful in a northern winter with 6-volt electrics, though Bedford engines were normally good starters.

The 2-ton and 30-cwt models altered so much in late 1935, not only in appearance but in overall construction, that it is surprising they were not given new designation letters. Here a Hull-based electricity company WHG short-wheelbase 2-ton model dating from early 1936 is being loaded with a cable drum from Derby Cables Ltd. The new vertically-slatted radiator was mounted further forward, much as on the WTL and WTB, but this model retained its normal-control layout, so even though the cab moved forward with the radiator and engine, the bonnet, now with horizontal louvres, remained quite long. The wheelbase was reduced by 11in to become exactly 10ft on this model. The cab became similar to that on the WTL in appearance but, being narrower, had a single windscreen. Overall, the effect was of a new model, even though the main mechanical units were little changed.

The 30-cwt WS was redesigned in the same fashion as the 2-ton models, and an early example, first registered in the North Riding of Yorkshire soon after the beginning of 1936, is seen working for a dairy in Middlesbrough. Note the traditional style of milk churn.

The 3-ton models continued almost unaltered from the form in which they had first gone into production in 1934, apart from the new radiator grille, and many operators well satisfied with early examples simply added more to their fleets. Here three 1935 WTH models are seen with a 1936 example, second from the right, in the fleet of contractor George C. Cross, of Iron Bridge, Southall, Middlesex. This address was very close to the AEC works, and although AEC, like other builders of heavier commercial vehicles, continued to build many vehicles for contractors, they undoubtedly lost business because of the sheer value for money of Bedford tippers such as these. Operating conditions for such vehicles were very harsh, and vehicle life was apt to be fairly short, but the WTH could earn its keep in hard work done during that time.

Another case of a WHG 2-ton van, with the main part of the body much as on the example on the old-style chassis shown on page 57, though with different cab, using the scuttle supplied with the 1936-type chassis. This time it was owned by Robinson's Fisheries, of Stratford, on the eastern outskirts of London. The Middlesex registration – perhaps by a dealer – dates it at the spring of 1936. Again one wonders why a 30-cwt was thought inadequate, and in this case carriage of fish in large quantities of ice may have been the answer. The shallow tank under the nearside of the body with filler at the front is curious – the normal fuel tank was on the offside. The number painted on the cab door related to what were called C-licences issued to operators who ran goods vehicles in connection with their own businesses as opposed to those who provided transport for others.

similar to the WT style, and the front axles were strengthened to suit the extra weight imposed on them. However, these lighter models did not have the semi-forward-control layout, so the bonnet became noticeably longer than on the 3-tonners. There were reductions in wheelbase length, by 11in to 120in (10ft) on the 30-cwt and short 2-ton model, and 14in to 143in (11ft 11in) on the long 2-ton model. Fuel tanks on all these models were carried on the frame side. With all these extensive changes it is surprising that the designation letters were not changed, for these were effectively new models.

The overall effect was of a more unified range of modern appearance, widely seen as overdue at the time, even though the dropping of the 'vintage'-style outline might be regretted by some nostalgic enthusiasts nowadays.

Remarkable though it may seem in these regulation-conscious days, the *Bedford Transport Magazine* of December 1935 was even more specific about the 'overload'

claim, reporting that "Bedford 2-ton, 3-ton and 30-cwt chassis (with approved body allowances) are guaranteed for a margin of 50-per cent over their respective nominal rated capacities". What it really meant was that Vauxhall's engineers had allowed for the cavalier attitude to nominal load ratings then common – bearing in mind the large numbers by then in service, this was quite a remarkable statement to make in such precise terms, reflecting great self-confidence which indeed was constantly being borne out in practice.

As with the previous generation of models, there was, even so, a demand for adaptations to allow Bedford chassis to be used to deal with heavier or bulkier loads, with six-wheel conversions or use of the short-wheelbase models, usually the WTH, as tractive units for articulated outfits.

Among the more remarkable of the six-wheelers was an adaptation of the WTL produced by Universal Power Drives Ltd, of Greenford, Middlesex, who traded as

The new-style WS 30-cwt model provided the basis for an up-to-date style of ambulance. This example had bodywork by Spurling, becoming adept at building neat-looking vehicles of smooth outline with well-executed details, such as the continuation of the waist moulding so as to line up with the pressing incorporated in the scuttle assembly. The small hubs continued as of old, but chromium-plated end caps gave a finished touch, and it went without saying that the radiator would be of the chromed type. This example had a Hull registration issued late in 1936, the prominent red cross on the roof possibly suggesting airport use at that date.

Unipower. It had a double-drive rear bogie, with twin tyres on both rear axles of the same 32x6 size as the standard model, and a two-speed auxiliary gearbox that, with the standard main gearbox, gave eight speeds in all. The wheelbase was extended to 14ft, measured to the centre of the rear bogie, and the overall length was 22ft 0in, the load capacity being increased to 6 tons. The Unipower bogie, with springs mounted on trunnions to allow operation over very uneven ground, cost £245, including chassis reinforcement and fitting, and the complete chassis cost £515.

The 12-cwt van now became the sole representative of the original Bedford outline, having changed from VYC and VXC to BYC and BXC on the adoption of the engines and synchromesh gearboxes of the B-series Big Six Vauxhall cars that had been in production for a couple of years – these were again overhead-valve sixes, the BYC unit being of 2,393cc and nominal 20hp, while the BXC had the familiar 3,180cc unit of 26.33hp, much as used in larger Bedfords. The radiator now became of the vertically slatted

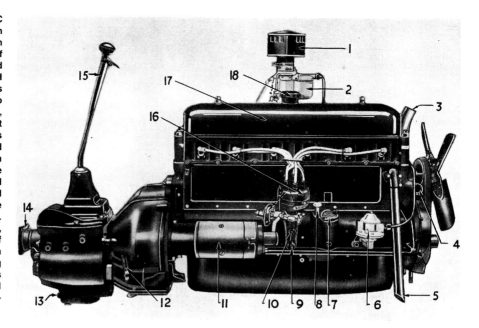

The '27hp' engine, really 26.33hp RAC rating, had not altered noticeably from the form in which it had first appeared in 1931, as shown on page 28. This view of an engine and gearbox is reproduced from the instruction book for 3-ton WTH and WTL and passenger WTB models issued in November 1936. The engine no longer has the sparking plug covers, deleted for the 1937 version. The most obvious difference from early engines was the downdraught carburettor, fitted above the inlet manifold rather than beneath it, and hence visible over the rocker cover in this view, as introduced for the WT range from 1934 and responsible among other changes for the increase of power to 64bhp at 2,800rpm. The gear lever, inclined forwards slightly, was to suit the semi-forward control of these models. Overall, as usual with Bedfords, it was quite a good-looking engine even though such matters probably were of no concern to the typical buyer of vehicles bought to do a down-to-earth job.

type and the external headlamp tie bar disappeared but the overall outline – in essence the 1929 Chevrolet, apart from minor details such as the wire wheels, now with larger chromed hub-caps, had become quite dated by late 1935. Yet, remarkably, it was to survive until the model was finally superseded in May 1939, though there was a notable mechanical change in the adoption of a three-speed gearbox in April 1938, derived from the Vauxhall 25hp car, model G, by then in production.

The more extensive design changes made across much of the range at the end of 1935 led to further widespread sales success without any need for further significant alteration until well into 1938 – by the end of

1937, sales of the Bedford range were exceeding 26,000 per year even excluding the light car-related vans.

That does not mean that there was a lack of activity in terms of design, even if signs of it were very modest to Bedford users – the sparking plugs on the 26.33hp engine, 'buried' under covers on the original design, became exposed from May 1936, there was a new forged steering connecting rod on the heavier models from November and in October 1937 models from the 12-cwt upwards had a cooling system thermostat added. Behind the scenes, a new engineering building, known as the V block, was added to the Luton premises in 1938, costing £175,000. It housed 335 engineers and attendant staff, and gave what were

The BYC 12-cwt van was really the previous VYC but with the engine from the Vauxhall 20hp Big Six car, with no more than the slatted radiator grille by way of visual change. This example for the surveyor's department of Southend Corporation looked a little more modern than most of the type by virtue of the design of its special bodywork, intended to carry both personnel and goods. Even so, it had more the look of a typical 1933 product than its actual date of registration in mid-1938. The performance with the standard engine was quite lively, but the BXC, with the 27hp engine, basically as shown above, was even more so, sometimes being chosen by newspaper proprietors in those days of keen competition to get the latest issue on to the streets without delay.

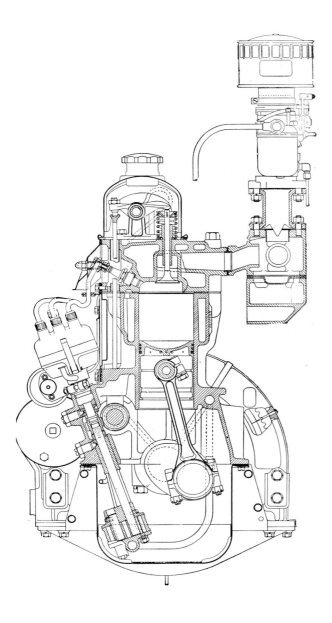

This sectioned view reveals the internal design of the 27hp engine in 1937 form – basically a straightforward 3.18-litre overhead-valve six-cylinder petrol engine, certainly built for economy in manufacture with such features as the pressed sump and rocker cover but more advanced than many commercial vehicle engines of its period. Noteworthy in this view is the dished shape of the piston crown. There were still many affinities to the 1929 Chevrolet 'Stove-bolt six' from which this unit was derived, though with the benefit of Vauxhall engineering quality in its pressure lubrication and four main bearings. There were no serious trouble spots and it would give reliable service over lengthy periods in widely varying types of duty. Even so, it was to be superseded by the even better-known 28hp, very similar in general concept but with many minor changes intended to improve efficiency, in July 1938.

claimed to be unrivalled facilities within Britain for the design and development of all types of vehicle.

By that time, the need to modernise and expand transport for the armed forces was beginning to become evident as the political situation in Europe was causing concern. Regular trials of motor vehicles for possible military use had been held since early in the century. During the 1914-18 war, nearly 2,000 of the Vauxhall D-type 25hp tourer had been built for the services, this model, together with the Sunbeam 12/16hp, being chosen as the standard staff cars for Army use. The Vauxhall gained a reputation for reliability and some of them were to be used in places where no car had ever been seen in the Balkans and the Middle East.

There had been only limited production of military vehicles in the early 1930s, most of it covered by traditional suppliers such as Thornycroft, Guy and, for the Royal Air Force, Crossley, though the military authorities were interested in developments from other concerns which might suit their needs. In the 1935 Army trials held at Llangollen, Bedford entered a 12-cwt van and a 2-ton lorry, the performance of the latter being recorded as particularly impressive. To better cope with arduous conditions, in the following year a slightly modified 2-ton vehicle, with 10.50-16 tyres to give better flotation over soft ground, was submitted with a 30-cwt load. However, in the 1937 event, also at Llangollen, a prototype 15-cwt of the MW type with square-nosed bonnet later to become familiar was entered, again performing extremely well. More detail on military types is given later, but suffice it to say here that the foundation of Bedford's major contribution to the 1939-45 was had been laid.

(continued on page 69)

Among the facilities of the new Vauxhall Engineering Research Building opened in 1938 were a number of giant-sized drawing boards, provided to allow full-scale layouts to be made to check preliminary work done on a smaller scale. Because paper is prone to vary in size with changes in temperature and humidity, creating variations of up to a quarter of an inch at such a size, cellulose-coated aluminium was used for these full-sized drawings. The draughtsman is shown at work with a small tee-square, but proper provision to ensure that lines were straight and true over the length and depth of the board would have been essential, even though this was before the days of drafting machines, let alone the modern techniques of computer-aided design.

Invited to take part in the War Department trials of vehicles with military transport potential in North Wales, Bedford obtained an encouraging degree of success in 1935 with standard 12-cwt and 2-ton models but in the 1936 event a modified WHG with 10.50-16 tyres carrying a 30-cwt test load performed well, making the fastest ascent of the Old Horseshoe Pass near Llangollen of all vehicles attempting it, other than cars. It also made an easy climb of Alt-y-Bady with a maximum gradient of 1 in 3.38. Here, although Bedford's engineers were quite happy with the engine cooling the Army engineers considered the temperature rise too great, so a modified fan was fitted and the bonnet altered slightly, giving the required result.

For the 1937 trial, a vehicle built to meet the Army's 15cwt specification with open cab was entered, though its mechanical design was based on the 2-ton model as used the previous year. Provisionally it was described as W.D.1, though it was effectively the prototype for the wartime MW 15-cwt Army truck to become familiar two years later. A very large military-style air cleaner specified by the Army would not fit under the standard bonnet, so a very simple square-nosed design was produced as a satisfactory answer for a one-off. It was not of quite the same design as later to become standard on Bedford wartime models, for which the large air-cleaner was not, after all, specified. Bedford planned to revert to the standard front-end, but the Army specifically requested the square nose. In those days, Army vehicles were registered in the normal way, taking Middlesex numbers and so 'W.D.1' was FMG 934. It is seen above storming up one of the hills in the 1937 trials, and climbing a grass-covered mountain track.

Output of Bedford vehicles for a wide variety of users continued to gain momentum in 1937. One of the more uncommon was this mines rescue van on a WS 30-cwt chassis placed in service early in the year by the Lancashire & Cheshire Coal Owners' Mines Rescue Station, at Boothstown, near Manchester. In those days, a decade before the setting-up of the National Coal Board, coal mines were run by quite a large number of proprietors, and this was one of a several co-operative ventures in which specialised rescue was provided jointly. Two Bedfords were operated, each combining the facilities of a normal ambulance with the carriage of specialised staff and equipment liable to be needed in the case of a mining accident. Breathing apparatus was carried for each man, together with tools and specialised rescue equipment.

The most typical Bedford continued to be a lorry, in this case a 2-ton WLG with platform body dating from the latter part of 1937 used by W. Daniel & Son Ltd, of Smithfield Market, Birmingham, which unlike its London namesake dealt in fruit and vegetables. The tall headboard allowed for boxes to be piled quite high if need be, and there was space behind the nameboard on the cab to house a folded tarpaulin.

Something quite different and unusual had been devised for the specialised needs of Thornton & Stimpson, seedsmen and nurserymen of Kingston-on-Thames. The heavier and more robust items could be loaded by hoist on the lorry section at the rear whilst smaller packages could be carried in the van section in front, the whole quite attractively shaped.

The sand and gravel pits of the Thames valley were home to numerous Bedford WTH tippers, such as this 1937 example of Folley Bros of Marlow and Sonning. It was probably quite new when photographed but the rear wheels and fuel tank begin to show the evidence of muddy ground and the steady drip of dirty water gradually shed by such loads. Note the presence of the BDC badge on many of the vehicles supplied to various types of user in this period.

Although the 'B' of WTB stood for 'bus', relatively few received bus bodywork as usually understood, the trend towards fitting Bedford chassis with coach-style bodywork even when intended largely for bus duties becoming very strong in the late 1930s. Among the exceptions was this example with Duple's standard but quite rare bus body for the model, still having much the same front-end as in 1935 though rather more rounded at the rear. This one registered in Salford in mid-1937 was purchased for use as a staff bus by the Lancashire Electric Power Company. The bus seems pretty full and one wonders whether the well-dressed group in the foreground might have been joining a staff outing, but perhaps in their own cars.

Bournemouth Corporation adopted the Bedford WTB as its standard single-deck type from 1937. This is one of the initial batch with Duple bodywork to a style based on the Hendonian design. After one repeat order, subsequent batches had Burlingham bodywork to very similar design.

Burlingham was one of several bodybuilders which built coach bodywork on the WTB chassis, even though none approached the numbers produced by Duple. This example was built in 1937 for Moore's Coaches of St Annes, better known as Lytham St Annes, only a few miles along the coast from Blackpool where the Burlingham premises were at Preston New Road. The vehicle had been taken to the impressive gates of Stanley Park for its official portrait. It had touches of this coachbuilder's designs built on larger forward-control chassis in 1935-6 in the pairing of windows with decoration applied to alternate pillars.

The original Duple Vista body for the WTB chassis created a combination of names that almost became part of the language of the typical coach operator. The characteristic feature was the combination of curved waist and roof lines with sloping pillars. The Scottish Motor Traction Co Ltd already a well-established Bedford user, chose the Vista for a batch of 30 WTB touring coaches in 1937. They had only 20 or 14 seats instead of the more usual 25 and were used for touring work, on which they were still to be seen well into the post-war period. This example, C93 (ASF 361) is seen in St Andrews Square, Edinburgh in the post-1948 green and cream livery, in company with a rebodied Leyland TS6.

Exports of virtually the whole Bedford range were strong from almost the beginning, and the WTB was no exception. This example, No. 23 in the fleet of Midland Luxury Lines, thought to be an Australian operator, had an extended wheelbase, such modifications of British commercial vehicle chassis being commonplace in that continent, where the dimensional regulations were less restrictive. The bodywork, with its high waistline and shallow windows, shows strong American influence, rather reminiscent of contemporary Greyhound coaches – the passenger seating level is well above that of the driver. The overall length looks as though it might have been about 30ft, well over the maximum 27ft 6in for a two-axle bus or coach in Britain at that date, and the seating capacity appears to be 28 on high-backed seats so the weight would doubtless be well up on a home-market model, slowing progress on hills, perhaps not a problem in many parts of Australia.

Willowbrook was another bodybuilder to produce a number of coach bodies on the WTB chassis, this one, believed to date from 1937-8, being typical. Despite its substantial appearance and high-backed seats, it weighed a modest 3tons 11cwt. It was built for W. Parsons of Stanton-under-Bardon, Leicestershire. This was not far from the bodybuilder's premises in Loughborough, though Wilowbrook was far from being merely a local bodybuilder, having a strong clientele, mainly among independent operators in those days, extending over most of the country.

A unique pair of WTB models was placed in service in 1937 by the Devon General Omnibus & Touring Co Ltd on a Torquay sea-front service. Although at first glance conventional 24-seat buses, they were unglazed at the sides, which accounts for the unusually low 2-tons 15cwt unladen weight – they must have been very lively, even if draughty, if the driver put his foot down, unlikely though that was

in normal use. The livery was a special duckegg blue, and the fleetname lettering was chromium-plated. They were stored during the war but rebuilt in 1946 for country service use, glazed and in Devon General's normal crimson and cream livery – they remained in use until 1954. Very unusually among 'provincial' vehicles at that date, they had bodywork by Birch Bros Ltd of Kentish Town, London, N.W.5, the old-established bus operators. That concern had to give up its services in London in 1934, as well as considerable bodybuilding for other London independents, after the setting-up of London Transport in 1933, though still running services into Bedfordshire and producing bodywork for its own vehicles. In the early 1920s, Birch had built many bodies for provincial companies in the major groups, although not itself connected with them, but this pair of vehicles seems to have been a one-off revival.

Despite the prominence given in contemporary publicity to the Duple Vista body, many operators favoured the same builder's Hendonian, also on the WTB but of slightly simpler design, with straight waist and vertical pillars, though offering much the same high standard of comfort within, in standard form. This tended to be particularly so with independent operators, who may have been influenced by the lower price, of £788 complete, in 26-seat form as compared to the £833 quoted for the 25-seat Vista II. That comparison might not be quite a fair one, for the Vista price included sliding roof and rear boot, not mentioned for the Hendonian, though very often fitted in fact.
David MacBrayne Ltd was an early Bedford user, purchasing WTB models every year from 1936 to 1939. The vehicle shown is believed to date from 1937, being one of a pair, 95-6 (AYS 3734), supplied as 25-seaters – others were largely 20-seat. The lettering in the window suggests that it may have been a show vehicle. In this case the use of slim chromium-plated pillars, usually on an alternate basis, has been arranged to give a row of three 'inter-connected' windows in the mid-section of the body, possibly as a show feature.

(continued from page 62)

The next development was a spin-off from a major venture by Vauxhall intended to further broaden its market appeal, in line with the strategy foreseen several years earlier by General Motors. This was the introduction of a new smaller car, this time a 10hp four-cylinder model, type H. Although smaller than any car built by Vauxhall since 1905, it continued to pursue the General Motors philosophy of being designed to compete in terms of its merits rather than on minimum price, even though this was very competitive. The development cost was £1 million, a fabulous sum in those days. It was of advanced design in being of integral construction – among the first in Britain – and having independent front suspension, the latter still

The 5/6-cwt HC-type van which first appeared in March 1938 was closely related to the Vauxhall Ten car introduced late in 1937, bringing advanced design and up-to-date appearance back to the Bedford van range. Outstanding fuel economy was reported, figures of well over 40mpg being attainable in non-stop running and around 33-35mpg in normal local delivery work. This example put on the road by a Swindon butcher a month or two later was given an eye-catching appearance by the choice of livery style, emphasising the convex-curve mudguards by then fashionable. Rear-hinged driver's and front passenger's doors had been usual on Vauxhall and Bedford bodywork since the beginning of the General Motors era.

This HC is of interest as an unusual case of a private lending library using a small van to take books to its borrowers, contrasting with the far more common use of larger vehicles by county library services to cover rural areas in later years. The location of Reids is not known, but the registration CWW 412 gives a strong clue that it was the West Riding of Yorkshire, as well as a Spring 1938 date. Here the standard van body was modified to provide a side service counter. The HC shared with the most basic 'loss leader' version of the Vauxhall Ten car the painted hub caps used instead of the chromed type found on most of the cars sold, but here a gold ring had been painted on them, doubtless by the signwriter.

very rare on cars of such size, though Vauxhall had introduced it on a revised Light Six range from the 1935 season. The overhead-valve engine, of 1,203cc, was designed by Alex Taub, who had returned to Britain after his career on engine design work for Chevrolet, in which he had become a specialist in efficient combustion, and the car could give 40mpg in normal service. Looking back at it from over half-a-century later, its three-speed gearbox seems a retrograde step, but this was in line with normal GM policy at the time, and less of a limitation in those days when a 60mph top speed was as much as could safely be sustained for long on most roads.

The new Bedford van appearing in March 1938 and derived from the Ten car was very conservatively rated as of 5/6-cwt capacity, being designated HC. It was the first four-cylinder Bedford, and the first to have independent front suspension. It also had thoroughly up-to-date appearance, of the type that could be important to say a

high-class florist, and which was more than could be said of the 8-cwt, still effectively a 1933 style, and looking it, and even more so the 12-cwt, with its boxy '1929 Chev' looks. The HC was also claimed to give 35mpg and at £140 was remarkable value.

Alex Taub's work was also evident at the other end of the range in July 1938, with a new engine to replace the 26.33hp unit which had served Bedford so well since 1931. The new engine was basically similar in being an overhead-valve six-cylinder unit, and only slightly larger in terms of capacity. It had $3\frac{3}{8}$in bore, just $\frac{1}{16}$th more than the previous unit, and 4in stroke, which was ¼in greater. This meant that the swept volume went up from 3,180cc to 3,519cc and the RAC rating became 27.34hp. Confusingly, it was common practice to round both RAC ratings up to 27hp for the 'old' engine and 28hp for the new one – this was in line with taxation practice in those days where cars were concerned.

The new '28hp' engine went with a new radiator grille, at first having the radiator filler under the bonnet and no more than a small fin-shaped decorative emblem on top. The changes in engine design altered its appearance only slightly and the combined effect is conveyed in this artist's impression of the front end of the WTB chassis in the form it was produced in its final year or so from July 1938. This drawing also conveys the way in which the semi-forward control layout common to the other WT models, still basically as devised by Stepney Acres in 1933, was laid out, although the artist's impression of the tyre size seems somewhat exaggerated.

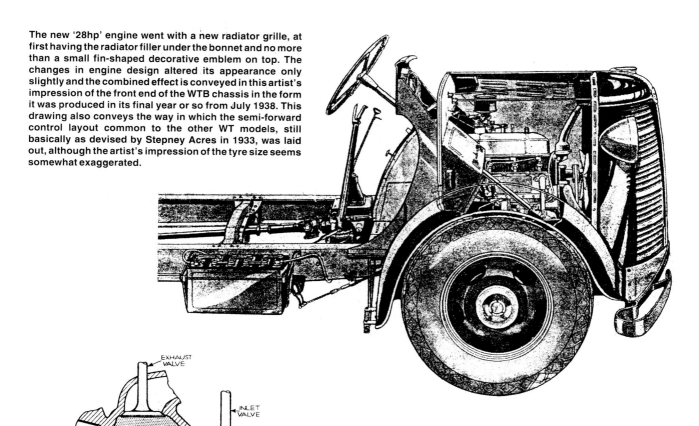

This diagram is a representation of the new type of combustion chamber devised by Alex Taub for the new 28hp engine. The piston, still cast iron – so, in effect, this engine could perhaps be described as 'grandson of cast iron wonder' – was no longer dished, and the relationship of valve positions to sparking plug was revised to give the controlled flame spread and improved efficiency sought. In practice the exhaust valve was slightly inclined to allow operation from the same rocker shaft as the inlet valve. Below, there were still four main bearings but the crankshaft now had counterbalanced webs, helping to make the engine smoother at speed and reducing stresses on bearings.

Power output went up, to 72bhp at 3,000rpm, by no means a huge increase, and on the road the general behaviour of the two engines was not noticeably different, at any rate to a passenger, with very quiet idling and smooth running at all speeds, with some induction roar as the throttle was opened. An improvement in torque allowed vehicles to be slightly higher geared, the WTB coach with the later engine having an axle ratio of 5.857 to 1 instead of 6.71 to 1, making the model less fussy at speed. Officially, such vehicles were not supposed to exceed 30mph, but twice that was by no means impossible if the police weren't about, and very few coaches of any type could improve on that in those days.

It is clear, however, that maximum power was not the primary aim. Taub was particularly interested in efficient combustion, and had developed a technique for measuring

how the flame front spread from the sparking plug through the petrol and air mixture in the cylinders. The new engine had what was called 'controlled flame' combustion chamber design, and while the phrase clearly owes a little to the advertising copy writer, it conveys the approach to this aspect of engineering. In conjunction with the design of Zenith caburettor, a lean mixture was provided for cruising conditions, and the idea of 'lean burn', much trumpeted as something new in recent years, was being pursued well over half a century ago in these engines, even if not in the sophisticated ways involving electronics possible today. This remarkable engine was not only to be the power unit for most of Bedford's models other than the car-derived vans until the early 1950s, but remained in production with few modifications until 1986, admittedly on a smaller scale in later years.

Also introduced in 1938 was a new style of radiator shell, with a more bowed shape and horizontal grille bars grouped in sets on each side of a vertical central strip. The bonnet sides were altered, with a set of horizontal bars to give an effect of continuity with the top set of grille bars. It had distinct echoes of Buick cars as introduced a year or so previously, a pattern that was also evident on Vauxhall cars. As before, the headlamps were supported from the grille, but now more directly, and the radiator filler cap was moved to an under-bonnet position. There were actually two versions of the grille, the type used on the long-bonneted WS 30-cwt and WHG or WLG 2tonners being less bowed in plan view than the version used on the WTH, WTL and the WTB coach chassis. Sometimes the latter types in particular were nicknamed 'bullnose' after the Morris cars of the 1920s, even though the overall effect was very different. In all cases it was intended that it should be

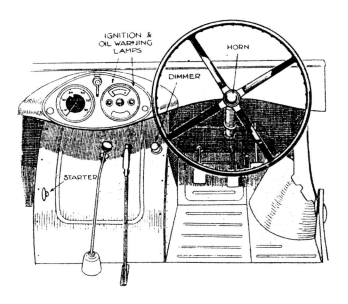

The driving position and controls were virtually unchanged on the 1938-9 WT-series models, though the style of instruments was discreetly modernised, being similar to those on contemporary Vauxhall cars. One tiny detail change was related to one of the few alterations in the layout of the 28hp engine by comparison with the 27hp unit. The starter was now on the left (kerb) side and as it was controlled by a switch on the unit itself, the starter pull was now on the left of the engine cover, as shown here, instead of in an equivalent position on the right as previously.

painted in the same colours as the bodywork, except for the chromium-plated decorative strips. Occasionally, in later years, the whole shell was plated, but the effect then was bordering on the vulgar.

Clearly it gave the impression to the casual observer of a new range, but effectively, apart from the new engine, the various models were as before. The distinctly 'American' look had its own appeal, though more effective when combined with appropriate bodywork, as on most coaches of the time. The standard Bedford cab of the time with flat windscreen (divided in the centre on the WTH and WTL), modern-looking though it had been when first seen on the original WT models of the 1934 season, did not blend too well with the new grilles. Once again, no changes to model designations were made. Quite unofficially, Omnibus Society members interested in vehicles christened the WTB with the new grille WTB2 for a time, but this was never recognised more generally.

A minor new addition to the range of standard factory products made at the same time was a hydraulically-operated tipper on the WTH chassis, priced at £330. Very slight price increases were made, the WTB chassis going up from £290 to £298, for example.

The new radiator sat a little uneasily on the front of the goods models, which retained the square-looking cabs from the previous types. These two 2-tonners of type WLG represent the third generation of model with that designation, which dated back to the beginning of Bedford production in 1931. The 1938-39 models also had the new 28hp engine so they were a transitional stage to the next generation of Bedford types in more than just radiator style. Renwick's was a firm of coal merchants in Bristol, the vehicle in the foreground, FHW 545, dating from early 1939, according to its registration number. Note the private owner railway coal wagons bearing the name Renwick Walton.

The WT types were perhaps slightly more attractive in the new form as introduced in mid-1938, partly because the bow-fronted radiator grille on these models was more rounded and hence the shape fitted more comfortably at the front of the sharply tapered bonnet, and also because the centre pillar of the divided windscreen provided a point of affinity with the chromium-plated centre strip of the grille. This WTH tipper of G. Dady, sand and gravel merchant, of Sydenham, was an early example of the type, having been registered in Croydon in the summer of 1938. Once again the pale blue Bedford Driver's Club badge is displayed.

For a few months in 1938-39, the 12-cwt BYC van continued in production unaltered alongside the larger models with their new-style radiator grilles, looking just as it had since 1935 and with a basic outline going back beyond the introduction of the VYC version in 1932 to the Chevrolet AC type. There had been a mechanical change from April 1938, to a three-speed gearbox as used in the contemporary Vauxhall 25hp car. This example, ARJ 818, was registered in Salford for Allied Dairies Ltd, Manchester, early in 1939 in the same registration batch as the two WS-type 30-cwt models in the background. The other BYC, RJ 5605, dated from 1936.

The new style of radiator and bonnet looked most at ease with modern coach bodywork, such as the latest Vista design, which had moved on to Vista III by the time of the 1938 Scottish Show, when a similar vehicle to this WTB was on display, though for the MacBraynes fleet and having 26-seat capacity. This one, with no owner's name shown, may have been built for demonstration duty – it appears to have seats for 25 passengers. The unladen weight is given as 3tons 13cwt, and bearing in mind the standard of comfort offered, with sliding roof and a very 'civilised' interior, modern designers might ponder why vehicles have become so much heavier.

The front view of a 1939-model Bedford WTB with Duple Vista body looked very up-to-date and stylish when new. The Vista body at that period had wider windscreens than used on the post-war version, a style of front-end inherited from the 1936 K.D. body design. In that initial year, the 'bull-nose' grille carried the headlamps at a higher level than familiar in the later version used on the OB, and there was only a small fin-shaped ornament on top, the radiator filler cap being under the bonnet. This is Southern National 479 (DDV 45), one of 28 similar 25-seat coaches placed in service in green and cream livery by the Southern National and Western National Omnibus Companies early in that year. Effectively, the two companies were run as one concern, except that they covered different areas of south-west England reflecting the fact that the respective railway interests in each were by the Southern Railway and the Great Western Railway. This accounts for the destination display, allowing one company to 'borrow' from the other as needs varied. Excursions and tours were an important activity and the two companies also operated the Royal Blue express services from London and the Midlands, on which these Bedfords were liable to appear, despite their green and cream colours, on summer week-ends. Bedford WTB coaches had been bought by SNOC and WNOC in 1937 and 1938, primarily for local coach duties, some of the SNOC vehicles being painted in a further livery, Scarlet Pimpernel, used for a time on North Devon tours.

The Duple Hendonian body continued to be the more popular type, especially among independent operators, in many parts of the country and although more restrained in its styling, also looked well with the new grille – sales were brisk, and for many such concerns one or two of these vehicles were to become the mainstay of the fleet for far longer than was expected, due to the war. On this design in 1939 form, the door was set further back and this allowed one seat to full luxury standard to be mounted ahead of it, but facing towards the driver, because the backrest would otherwise have obstructed the entrance – see the internal view on the opposite page. A similar arrangement was found on some 1939 Vista bodies but using a less bulky and more bus-like seat. With six rows of forward-facing seats and the one at the centre of the rear row, this brought the total to 26, thus getting the full value for the 26-seat step in the licence fee. The example shown was for Deacon & Hardy, Barlestone, Leicestershire, and was also noteworthy for the optional metal visor over the windscreen, perhaps marginally helpful when driving towards the sun but clashing somewhat with the smooth body outline and doing nothing for the air-flow over it – perhaps not important if the speed was kept down to the legal 30mph.

The Western Welsh Omnibus Co Ltd took delivery of these twelve WTB buses in the latter part of 1938, the vehicle nearest the camera being No.473 (BBO 305). They are lined up outside the factory where they, like thousands of Bedford passenger chassis over the years, were bodied – the Hendon premises of Duple Bodies & Motors Ltd, as the company then was. The office block in the background had been newly built that year, and an effective publicity picture resulted, even though bus bodies represented only a minority of the company's output at the time. For this order, the bus body structure was given a front-end like a Hendonian body, though with the rectangular Clayton destination box. The entrance had a folding door and the seating capacity was reduced to 20, this being the maximum for one-man operation at this time.

This interior view of a WTB with Duple Hendonian body dating from 1938-9 is typical in many respects of Bedford coaches of the late pre-war period. A total of 2,320 WTB models had been built when production ceased in the summer of 1939, and many were much like this. The substantial seats, quite elaborately trimmed, were typical of the period and, with a sliding roof, the overall standard of comfort for passengers was high. The good riding qualities of the chassis and smooth engine, virtually inaudible when idling, were important elements in this. When moving off, or on hilly terrain, the gearbox would make itself heard – road test reports in those days rarely made outright criticisms, but P. M. Sanders, writing in *Bus & Coach* in November 1938, observed that 'the indirect gears could not be recommended for quiet running', although he could 'speak only highly of the general road behaviour of the vehicle'. Laden to 5 tons gross, equivalent to not far short of a full load, 14 miles were run on a 1-gallon test tank over a difficult course. The Hendonian body had a narrower windscreen design than the Vista, with angled windows on each side, and although this did not quite give as broad a view forward as from the Vista, this did not materially affect the driver, since he sat fairly close to the screen and had a good view over the very short bonnet. The controls were conveniently placed, and the passengers, as well as the driver, had a good view of the speedometer, of particular interest to small boys, this vehicle having the revised instruments used with the new radiator style. The position of the entrance did not allow the bulky single passenger seat ahead of it to face forward, and the sideways position was hardly ideal, the passenger having to sit at a very uncomfortable angle to see forward, and in addition, the driver's view to the nearside at road junctions must have been restricted by it. Note the guard to prevent the gear lever being inadvertently moved by a passenger.

Exports were an important part of Bedford's business, even in pre-war days. This 'line-up' was a fake, but a fleet of 32 WTB models with Duple 26-seat bus bodywork to the design shown was supplied to the Anglo-Iranian Oil Company in 1939.

All too few of the new O-series goods models put into production in the summer of 1939 were to have no more than a few months of service with their initial owners, for large numbers were compulsorily acquired for use by the Army at the outbreak of war in 1939. Some are thought to have been left behind in France when the British Expeditionary Force was evacuated from Dunkirk, minus its vehicles or tanks, and these were mostly deliberately destroyed. One dating from 1939 that might have escaped such a fate was this OL long-wheelbase 3- to 5-ton model, on which Duple built the special body shown and, it seems, part of the cab, though this incorporated the new-style windscreen and conformed fairly closely to the new standard style. The body would have made it of less interest to the military authorities.

This vehicle apparently photographed early in 1939, was evidently a prototype for the OB, on which Duple had built what would have been the 1940 version of the Hendonian body style which had proved particularly popular on the WTB with independent operators. The wheelbase is recorded as 14ft 6in, which in itself identifies the chassis as of OB type, but another key feature of the type is, in effect, almost literally highlighted. This was the external radiator filler, adopted after the concealed 1938-9 type had proved unpopular, and here the filler cap sits noticeably higher above the radiator cowl than on production models. The body retained the straight waist and vertical pillars of earlier Hendonian models, but the windscreen was of vee-type, thus conforming to the style of the new goods range.

# 6  A CLEAN SWEEP OF NEW MODELS

Although the international situation was becoming ominous, the earlier part of 1939 was a time of great activity on new products for Bedford's normal customers, with almost the whole range of models replaced by new, only to be abruptly swept away by the outbreak of war on 3rd September and a rapid switch to military needs.

The year started fairly quietly with the introduction of a rather unusual wood-bodied pick-up version of the 10hp HC van in January, called the Utility Wagon. The Vauxhall Ten car, from which the HC was derived, was of integral construction, but a chassis version was built for other bodies. It was rated at 6 cwt, rather than the 5/6 cwt quoted for the van, which may have been because it genuinely was capable of carrying a little more but might have been a sign of realisation that the van rating had been rather misleading; the little 750cc Austin Seven had been rated at 5 cwt in van form and other makers' 5-cwt models were also smaller, being based on cars of 8-hp rating. A quite different design with a title which was apt to be confused with it was the Utilecon, a name adopted by Martin Walter for what amounted to an estate car version of the smaller Bedford van models.

Articulated Bedfords had been used in modest numbers since the earliest days, but a new venture announced in the Spring of 1939 was the first purpose-built Bedford-Scammell, an interesting episode of co-operation with another commercial vehicle maker, quite independent, producing a combination which filled gaps in both makers' quite different ranges. The basic idea was to fit the same type of automatic coupling gear to a short-wheelbase Bedford 2-ton or 3-ton chassis as was used on the Scammell Mechanical Horse, the latter being the three-wheeled tractive unit that had become popular, especially with railway companies, as a means of hauling semi-trailers. The coupling gear and semi-trailers were made by Scammell and the Bedford chassis were fitted with special rear springs so as to ensure that the coupling height was within the limits needed for the automatic pick-up system to work satisfactorily.

Most of the Mechanical Horse units were used over short distances in urban areas – indeed, as the name implied, replacing the horse and cart, of which the railway companies still had many thousands, especially in the larger cities. Quite deliberately, Scammell had not aimed at high performance, and the Mechanical Horse was built in two forms, the 3-ton model with an 1,125cc engine and the 6-ton model with a 1,970cc unit, both side-valve four-cylinder, developing 20bhp and 40bhp respectively. They

The 5/6-cwt HC was the only model included in the range at the beginning of 1939 that was to remain in production after a spate of new models announced in June. There was a minor styling change applied to Vauxhall car models and their van derivatives which identifies this example as a 1939 model, this being the style of bumper with single groove instead of the multiple grooving of the 1938 series. The body is thought to be an early variation of the 'Utilecon' design introduced by Martin Walter of Folkestone, Kent, hitherto a specialist in drop-head or cabriolet car bodies, largely on Vauxhall chassis. This was a revival of the idea of the single vehicle that could carry passengers or goods that had been built in small numbers as a variation of the early VYC 10/12-cwt van. The standard version used the van doors at the rear for passenger access, except for the normal driver's and front-seat passenger's doors. This four-door version was described as a 'Shooting Brake', or what later would be called an estate car, a body style then quite rare in Britain. Although the American version of the idea, notably the Ford V8 'Woody', was beginning to gain favour on a limited scale on this side of the Atlantic, that was a larger and much more costly type of vehicle to run and aimed at a more upmarket type of clientele.

The Bedford-Scammell, in its original form, had hardly been introduced early in 1939 before it became obsolete, being the last type to appear with the 'square' cab. Seen here is an example based on the WHG short-wheelbase chassis, basically a 2-ton model, which could haul a 6-ton load when much of the payload weight was carried on the semi-trailer's rear axle, though the tractive unit had special springs in addition to the Scammmell automatic coupling gear. This example, JMT 536, was supplied to Hoppings of Whetstone, timber merchants, based on the northern outskirts of London. Note how both Bedford and Scammell names appeared on the radiator grille, using the style of lettering adopted when the 'bull-nose' grille appeared the previous year. However, the development work had not been lost, for an updated version of the Bedford-Scammell formed part of the new range, as well as being taken up slightly later as a basis for various wartime models.

could certainly outperform a horse but not by an enormous margin; trundling along at about 15-20mph was about their mark, not unsatisfactory in slow-moving urban traffic for the purpose for which they were mainly intended, but not for greater distances or up prolonged steep gradients.

The roles foreseen for the Bedford versions included being able to pick up the same type of semi-trailer as handled by the Scammell, possibly even the same actual units, and haul them where more power, better braking and the greater stability of a four-wheeled tractive unit would be of value. Two versions were offered, based on the WHG which could tackle the 6-ton semi-trailer as used with the Mechanical Horse, and the WTH-based model which could go up to an 8-ton payload and a gross weight for the complete outfit of up to 12 tons. Ironically, few of these versions were built before the WHG and WTH were superseded by new models, but the Bedford-Scammell link had been established and was to be of great value during the war and afterwards.

The apparent under-rating in terms of load capacity of the 5/6cwt HC van was certainly avoided on the next new

model to appear, which looked very similar and not much larger and yet had twice the load rating. This was a new 10/12-cwt van, the JC – it had the engine of the then new Vauxhall Twelve-Four car, model I, very similar in design to the Ten, but with bore increased from 63.5mm to 69.5mm on the same stroke of 95mm and a 1,442cc capacity. However the structure of the JC van was not derived from the I-model car but the J, a new integral construction Fourteen-Six of which the engine (the old but still very effective Light Six unit) was not now being offered in a Bedford model. The J-type underframe and suspension gave the basis for a model with 105in (8ft 9in) wheelbase, usefully larger than the HC, though having a close resemblance to it in general appearance. The standard van body was also a little taller and as the front-end styling, including the door pressings, was common to the two models, the roof swept up rather more sharply from the windscreen – in other respects they were not easy to distinguish.

At last, Bedford had an up-to-date and cohesive small van range. The old 8-cwt AS-series as built since 1933 and

The new 10/12-cwt van, type JC, introduced in 1939, looked like a mildly enlarged version of the 5/6-cwt HC first seen the previous year, and was considerably lighter than the BYC-type van it replaced, weighing 18cwt unladen rather than 24cwt, but it was also far more up-to-date. The engine was of 1,442cc, with four cylinders, incorporating Alex Taub's ideas on efficiency, instead of an older design of 2,392cc six-cylinder, and with the lighter build there were major gains in fuel economy without much loss in performance, especially when lightly loaded, as delivery vans often are. With one relatively minor redesign which did not alter appearance, a van of this general pattern was to survive in the Bedford range until 1952.

the BYC 10/12-cwt, of even older outline, had finally gone. The new 10/12-cwt was of much lighter general concept than the BYC, and with a smaller engine having two fewer cylinders, but its much more modern design, with independent front suspension, still rare on a delivery van, made it more appealing to most users.

The JC van was just one of a whole new Bedford range announced in June 1939, which left only the small HC van, itself announced only the previous year, continuing from what had gone before. What was more, the familiar model designations, some of them going back to 1931, were also to vanish, although in its usual way, Bedford stuck to weight ratings in its publicity material for the new models. There was obvious continuity, and most of the new features first seen in the 1938 revamp, such as the 'bullnose' radiator and the 27.34hp six-cylinder engine, carried over

into the new range. Indeed, look a little deeper, and many other familiar features were still there.

There were new weight ratings, stretching from a 30/40cwt up to a 5-ton model, the latter taking Bedford much further into what had been the 'heavy' vehicle makers' territory. Most obvious to the casual observer, there was a completely new pressed steel cab, with more rounded shape and divided windscreen with the two panels having radiused corners and set at a slight vee angle. The effect was reminiscent of the Fisher 'turret top' car bodies fitted to the various marques of General Motors cars in America from 1936, although its styling was more restrained. The combined effect, with the bull-nose radiator, looked 'all-of-a-piece' and it was now possible to realise that the rather unsatisfactory combination of this grille style with the old 'square' cab was no more than an interim stage. Although

The Utilecon version of the 10/12-cwt JC van was to become quite a familiar sight, offering seats for 7 passengers and yet being capable of conversion to goods carrying 'in 30 seconds'. The Royal Navy took to the type, and examples were to be seen on the streets of most seaports during the war years and for some time thereafter.

The K-type 30/40-cwt, as built from June 1939

The WS-type 30-cwt, as built July 1938 to May 1939

The ML-type 2/3-ton, as built from June 1939. MS-type similar but shorter.

The WLG-type 2-ton, as built July 1938 to May 1939. WHG-type similar but shorter.

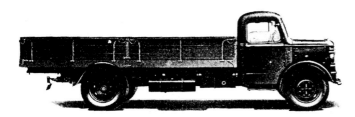

The OL-type 3/4-ton, as built from July 1939. OS-type similar but shorter. The 5-ton versions of each, with '/40' suffix, looked almost identical.

The WTL 3-ton, as built July 1938-May 1939. WTH-type similar but shorter. No 5-ton version.

modern and having some clear indications of Detroit influence, the overall effect had a functional and quite 'British' character of its own.

The relationship of the new models with their predecessors can best be set out in tabular form.

| New model | Rating | Previous model | Rating | Identification |
|---|---|---|---|---|
| K | 30/40-cwt | WS | 30-cwt | Single rear tyres |
| MS & ML | 2/3-ton | WHG & WLG | 2-ton | Long bonnet |
| OS & OL | 3/4-ton | WTH & WTL | 3-ton | Short bonnet |
| OS/40 & OL/40 | 5-ton | - | - | Short bonnet (helper springs at rear) |

Further letters were added to indicate the type of body, such as D for dropside lorry.

There were some general changes in the new range, notably the adoption of hydraulic operation of the brakes, in conjunction with a servo on models of 2/3-ton rating and over – there were separate hydraulic circuits for front and rear brakes to guard against a hydraulic failure disabling the whole system. The handbrake, also revised, was now sited between the front seats, having more of a pull-up action. The under-bonnet radiator cap of the 1938 models had been widely criticised and it now appeared in the traditional place on top of the radiator shell in place of the small 'fin' – the new cap was chromium-plated and rounded in shape and, to some observers at least, suited the overall design rather better. Also, the headlamps were lowered to almost half-way down the radiator shell, thus being mounted slightly below the level of the sidelamps.

On the other hand, there was a great deal that was familiar, some of it going right back to 1931 or, indeed, the Chevrolet era. On the K 30-cwt, there were still the Chevy-

The star of the new goods range of June 1939 was the 5-ton model, seen here in long-wheelbase dropside form, of which the full designation at that date was OLD/40. The new pressed-steel cab with vee-shaped windscreen matched the front-end styling of the chassis almost perfectly, producing what must surely rank as one of the all-time classics of design among commercial vehicles. It and indeed the whole new range also lived up to the motto 'What looks right, is right' in the sense of being thoroughly practical vehicles that gave good service to thousands of users. Although many of the examples added to operators' fleets in the summer of 1939 were requisitioned for military use on the outbreak of war in September that year, the type was destined to become a familiar sight on Britain's roads again within months of the resumption of production in 1945, and within a year or two the old motto 'You see them everywhere' applied to this family of Bedford models in particular. Although the overall design was still clearly related to Stepney Acres's WT trend-setter that had gone into production in 1934, some quite extensive detail redesign had occurred, for example in the wheels and hubs. The 1939 price of £345 complete with body of the model shown must have caused considerable concern to makers of traditional-style heavy-duty models, into whose 'territory' it encroached more closely than hitherto while costing less than half of the chassis price of the cheapest AEC, for example, the latter admittedly an 8-ton model.

style disc wheels with projecting hubs. Throughout the range, the gearbox was still the familiar old unit with sliding-mesh engagement of the straight-toothed gears for all indirect ratios, virtually as introduced in 1931 and unaltered in its wailing tone. Even in 1939, it was becoming quite old-fashioned and yet it was to soldier on for another decade – indeed, along with the engine, both units were yet to be built in far greater numbers even than before. Like the rest of the design, it was remarkably tough, and gave very little trouble.

The altered weight ratings could, in some respects, be regarded as a tacit endorsement that the previous ones allowed for a margin of overloading. Society was becoming less easy-going on such matters and probably it would no longer have been wise to imply that overloading was regarded as acceptable. The new 5-ton model went a little

The key difference of the 5-ton models which distinguished them from the very similar-looking 3/4-ton O-types was the addition of helper springs over the rear axle, taking part of the extra load. The rear tyre size also went up from 32x6 to 34x7, at first at the rear only, but later the larger size was standardized all round.

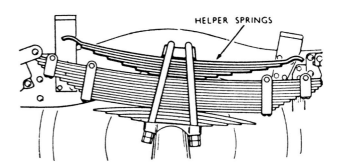

This nearside view of the engine in a 1939 5-ton model shows that it still had much the same general appearance as that in the earlier types, going back to the WT models of 1934. A new feature was the by-pass oil filter attached to the manifolds at a level making attention as simple as possible. The engine's compression ratio at this stage was over 6 to 1, high by contemporary standards, especially for a unit intended to run on 'commercial' petrol, but smoothness of running was, if anything, even better than with the earlier Bedford six-cylinder engines.

further than a 50% overload on the 3ton model from the previous range – which would have implied 4tons 10cwt – and among design changes were the addition of helper springs over the main rear springs, to come into operation as the weight was increased, and a change to 34x7 tyres on the rear axle – those at the front remained of 32x6 size.

Even so, there was still an indication that the advertised load rating was not the maximum the chassis would stand – a published maximum gross laden weight of 8 tons 14 cwt allowed almost a ton over the actual weight of a dropside long-wheelbase lorry carrying 5 tons and crew of two. The wheelbase lengths were as on the 3-tonner, with the familiar 157in (13ft 1in) for the long-wheelbase version. The chassis price was £295.

A road test carried out on an OLD/40 dropside 5-ton model by *The Commercial Motor*, as reported upon in its 4th August 1939 issue, spoke highly on almost all aspects of its behaviour, with particular praise for the smooth running engine and the brakes, no longer criticised for being over-servoed – indeed the only criticism made was that the helper springs, at the loading of exactly five tons being carried, were only just in contact with the frame and tended to clank against the abutments on rough sections of road. The vehicle weighed 2 tons 9 cwt unladen and thus was still within the '30mph' class.

To cater for the extra weight, the rear axle ratio was 6.83 to 1 instead of the 5.86 to 1 of a 3-ton model tested on 26th August 1938; this brought maximum speed down from 55mph to 50mph. Over quite a hilly route, fuel consumption of the 5-tonner worked out at 12.65mpg at an average speed of 28mph. In view of several spells on hills at down to 11mph, this indicates that, naughtily but realistically, at times it must have been travelling at well over the 30mph laid down by law for a vehicle of this type anywhere in those days, and hence was by no means a test rigged to give a favourable figure. Fuel consumption of the 3-tonner had been 16.6mpg, but possibly a more interesting comparison was with the early WTL model test report dated 3rd August 1934, which returned 12.6mpg over a similar route. In other words, the new model was as economical to run as that vehicle, despite carrying 5 tons instead of 3 tons, a clear measure of the greater efficiency of the later engine.

By that date, diesel engines were firmly established in Britain for heavier types of vehicle, sometimes saving up to half the fuel consumed compared to equivalent petrol models. However, their first cost was much higher and the weights of such vehicles themselves mostly considerably greater, putting them well over the 2 tons 10 cwt weight limit and making their maximum legal speed 20mph as well as swallowing some of the fuel saved in pulling themselves around. Diesel engines for smaller vehicles were being made, notably by Perkins, but their cost was considerable; none of the car and truck volume makers considered it worthwhile offering such an option on a production basis and conversions were still rare.

The new bus and coach chassis, the OB, introduced several important new features. The wheelbase was increased by 7in to 174in (14ft 6in), the overall length of the chassis being 24ft 1⅛in, increasing to about 3in more with bodywork. The frame had a slightly more marked drop in level between the axles and at the rear whilst a new feature was the offsetting of the spiral bevel unit, now with a 6.17 to 1 ratio, to the nearside to allow a lower centre gangway level. The laden frame height was 1ft 11⅝in. In practice, floor level was almost always rather higher than the minimum possible.

This is understood to have been the last of the new range to go into production, barely started before war broke out in September 1939. Only 73 had been built when production was stopped as wartime needs took priority, and of these the largest groups to enter service with operators in Britain are believed to have been the eight for the Western National Omnibus Co Ltd and ten for the Southern National Omnibus Co Ltd which entered service with those inter-related fleets in 1940 They had Duple Vista bodywork not unlike the post-war pattern but seating only 25, the same as this operator's coaches on WTB chassis. Others did reach various independent operators, including one with a 26-seat Thurgood bus body for B. Mandale, of Greystoke, near Penrith, in Cumberland.

The chassis numbers indicate that 9,856 of the K, M and O series goods and passenger chassis were built between June 1939 and 1940 before production of these series of models stopped completely until after the end of the war.

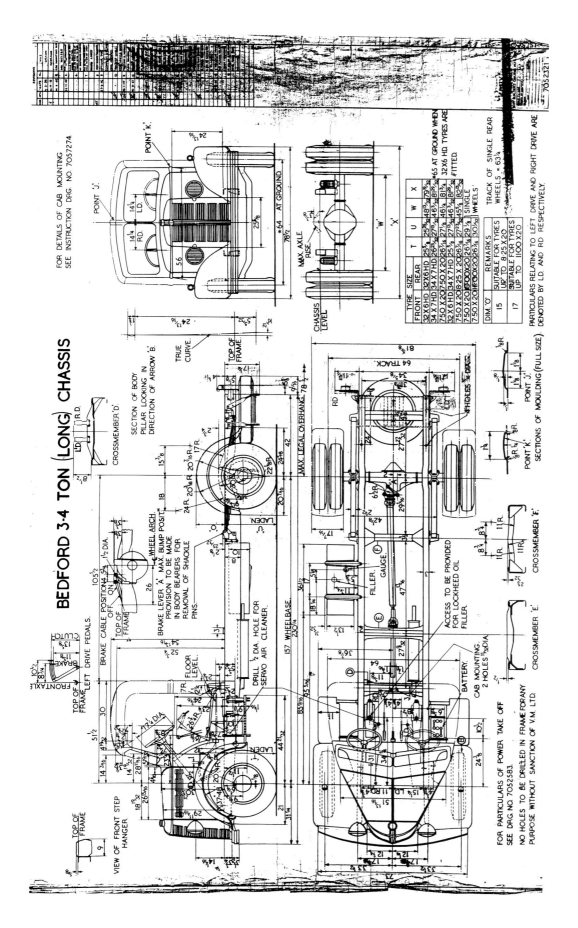

# BEDFORD 3·4 TON (LONG) CHASSIS

This bodybuilder's drawing of the OL-series 3/4-ton long chassis was originally drawn in March 1939, though redrawn in November 1945 as resumption of civilian production resumed. Various other additions cover alternatives such as optional tyre sizes made available over the years. Rather surprisingly, the one drawing was used for both right- and left-hand steering versions, and where this affects the design, the marks RD and LD indicated the differences – for example the rear lamp and registration bracket was provided on one side only, as appropriate. The dotted outline of the cab appears accurate in the side view but appears to have been simplified somewhat in the front view.

The original OB chassis, as introduced in 1939, was quite extensively revised in design, as compared to the WTB. The frame was described as more of a true passenger model, with the frame lowered to a greater degree, requiring quite a pronounced 'kickup' over the rear axle. The rear axle final drive gears and differential were offset to the nearside, to allow the gangway to be relatively low, but in practice these features were rarely if ever exploited to the full; most bodybuilders preferred to build bodywork with a high enough floor level to allow seats to face forward over the rear wheels. Apart from the features common to the other mid-1939 models, such as the return to an external radiator filler cap and the lower-mounted headlamps, this view shows this model's handbrake position, to the right of the driver, using a 'pull-upwards' lever mounted on a frame outrigger, with the cable leading diagonally through a hole in the frame to the linkage on the rear axle. The model had only just got into production when the war began, it being understood that 73 OB chassis were built in 1939, of which 40 were sold to British users. The immediate demands of war production on Bedford were such that civilian bus or coach chassis production ceased virtually as soon as war broke out, unlike most makers of heavier bus models which were able to continue on a limited scale, until the later part of 1940. However, from 1942, what amounted to the same model with only minor changes to meet wartime requirements, notably military-style headlamps and the elimination of chromium-plated trim, resumed production as the OWB, and manufacture of the OB proper resumed, reverting to the original design, at the end of 1945.

Only small numbers of the new OB model entered service in 1939-40. Thought to have been the largest fleet in Britain was the ten for Southern National Omnibus Co Ltd of which No. 495 (DOD 544) is seen here in post-war days, in company with a visiting Crossley coach. The Duple Vista bodywork was to have been the 1940 standard for the type, and shows an interesting blend of a rear-end like earlier Vista designs with a new front using a vee windscreen layout. The latter, with radiused corners at top and bottom and larger in size than adopted post-war, was perhaps more stylish than the familiar later version.

A rather surprising development was the reappearance of Chevrolet on the British market in 1939, when General Motors opened a plant in Southampton to deal with imported Chevrolet and Opel models, The latter built up a limited following in Britain for a time despite the growing political tension. The standard Chevrolet was broadly comparable to the Bedford 2/3-ton ML series in being of normal-control layout. The engine was still the 'cast iron wonder' six-cylinder overhead-valve unit, though it had also gained some benefit from Alex Taub's work before he returned to Britain, gaining a new four-bearing bottom end, and thus becoming comparable with the Bedford unit in this respect, yet it still had splash-lubricated big-ends, by then regarded as obsolete in Britain. The radiator grille was not unlike the Bedford version in general shape, in accord with General Motors' contemporary ideas on styling, though with slats evenly spaced, but the front mudguards were more rounded. Duple built the coachbuilt cab with obvious resemblences to the Bedford pressed-steel cab, though the proportions, shorter and with a more upright look than the latter, did not match the 'streamlined' front-end of the chassis as happily as was achieved on the Bedford version. The chassis price of the Chevrolet in 2-ton long form was £258, making it a little dearer than the equivalent Bedford in Britain, and it seems likely that the coachbuilt cab and body built in relatively small numbers would have been out more expensive than the mass-produced Bedford products.

An even more rare sight in Britain was this 1939 Chevrolet 'Cab Over' truck, again with Duple cab, though in this case the supply of the chassis maker's windscreen assembly as part of the chassis meant that the overall profile was much nearer to the standard transatlantic product. Possibly meant for re-export in view of the left-hand drive, it may have been fitted with British cab and body for an Empire market. The British form of forward control, with driver alongside the engine, was never taken up in the United States, though the cab-over-engine layout had been used there for some commercial vehicles since before the First World War. Inevitably it implied a higher overall build, and here two external steps are provided. Although the bonnet length was probably not much different from that of a WT- or O-series Bedford, the view forward over so high a snout must have been limited, especially when manoeuvering in tight spaces. Driving it in Britain would have been particularly difficult, and a phrase for such cabs coined by one observer of the commercial vehicle scene was 'lighthouse'. The overall appearance would have been helped by the addition of a front bumper, provision for the brackets of which can be seen at the base of the front cowl; it may have been removed to reduce dimensions for shipping purposes.

## A German dimension

Competition from General Motors's German subsidiary, Opel, in which a controlling interest had been acquired in 1929, was another factor in the rather complex picture of the late 1930s. It was a larger concern than Vauxhall, even though relatively small by General Motors standards. In the light of the outbreak of war in September 1939, the sale of Opel commercial vehicle chassis in Britain at that time seems more strange in retrospect than it did at the time. Imports of German cars, among which one of the most popular was a small Opel model, were not uncommon in Britain in the late 1930s, and although those of commercial vehicles were more limited, General Motors tended to encourage its subsidiaries to open up markets wherever they could, and the German Government was keen to earn foreign currency. A 2½-ton truck had been marketed in Britain from 1935, sales being handled via Oldsmobile and Opel Distributors Ltd, based in Fulham, London, S.W.6. It had a 3,485cc side-valve six-cylinder engine which had American origins revealed by its $3\frac{1}{8}$in bore and $4\frac{5}{8}$in stroke, but that model was extremely rare in Britain. It was, in fact, an Oldsmobile design.

By 1937, an overhead valve six with metric dimensions of 90mm bore and 95mm stroke and 3,626cc capacity had been adopted for a new 3-ton model, with several family similarities to the Bedford designs, though the five-speed gearbox, with helical gears making fourth almost silent, was very different from the Bedford unit. This was marketed in Britain, as well as a coach chassis, and modest sales successes were achieved. Opel used the name 'Blitz' for its commercial vehicles, and again in retrospect that took on sinister overtones in Britain, yet its direct meaning was simply 'Lightning' – oddly enough, a highly respected British maker, Thornycroft, had used Lightning as a model name for a lively six-cylinder coach model in the late 1920s, and Opel's intended implications were doubtless just the same. Unfortunately for this quite innocent image of speed, the technique of the German army as was to be demonstrated in 1940 was of what was called the 'Blitzkrieg' or lightning war, very much as adopted by the Croatian army in August 1995. In Britain in 1940-41, the word became extended to mean aerial bombing, so 'The Blitz' often meant the bombing of cities, especially London.

When war did come, the supply of Opel chassis ceased abruptly, but they were soon to become a familiar sight on the battlefield, for the German army relied on the model as its principal 3-ton truck just as the British army was to do with the Bedford. The Opel works was seized by the German Government on the outbreak of war, but it was ironic that two trucks having many similarities and both derived from the work of General Motors designers, even though with considerable input by their respective makers, should be such important means of transport for the opposing armies in Europe and North Africa. The story of the huge contribution to the British war effort of Bedford trucks and Vauxhall Motors generally forms the subject of the next Chapter.

**Left:** The standard Opel truck and coach chassis front-end of the late pre-war and wartime period was nearer to the Bedford version of the 1936-38 period, with vertical-slatted radiator, though this had the different outline shown and was mounted in a slightly sloping position.

**Below left:** On opening the bonnet of an Opel, anyone familiar with a Bedford would immediately find their way about without difficulty, as no doubt must have happened many times during the war with examples captured from German army units. No doubt the reverse was also true for an Opel driver or mechanic confronted with a captured Bedford. Even the rocker cover had that typical Chevrolet-based outline.

**Below:** For comparison, this is a typical Bedford 28hp engine and gearbox assembly, from a 2-ton model judging by the gear-lever shape. The downdraught carburettor, with cylindrical air-cleaner above, dynamo and starter are all in the same position as on the Opel unit shown on the opposite page.

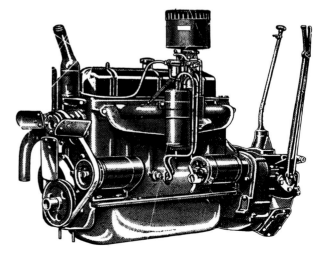

# The Heart of a Truck

**COMMERCIAL MOTOR SHOW EARLS COURT STAND NO. 110**

The *OPEL TRUCK ENGINE* will appear familiar to truck owners and drivers. Made to a specification which has been proved for many years, and improved year by year, it is the trusty friend and unfailing servant of its owner.

### ENGINE SPECIFICATION.

**ENGINE.** 6-cylinder, overhead valve type. Bore 90 m.m. (3.54"). Stroke, 95 m.m. (3.74"). Cubic Capacity, 3,626 c.c. (221.3 cu. inches). R.A.C. Rating, 30 h.p. 79 b.h.p. Maximum torque, 175.1 ft.-lbs. **CYLINDERS,** Cast en bloc integral with upper half crankcase; of special heat treated alloy. **CRANK-SHAFT.** Drop forged treated steel fitted with harmonic balancer. **CAMSHAFT.** Drop forged heat treated steel, hardened and ground. **VALVES.** Inlet valve of heat treated chrome molybdenum steel; exhaust valve of silichrone steel. Entire valve mechanism enclosed in the steel oilproof covers. **LUBRICATION.** Pressure feed lubrication to all main bearings, connecting rod bearings, gudgeon pins, camshaft and rocker arm shaft bearings. **ELECTRICAL EQUIPMENT.** Bosch 6-volt Starting and Lighting Equipment. **COOLING SYSTEM.** Centrifugal water pump gear driven. **FUEL SYSTEM.** Opel Down draught carburetter, fitted with accelerator pump; air cleaner.

# OPEL
## (UNDER 50 CWT.)
# 3 TON TRUCKS

| OPEL 3 TON TRUCK PRICES | | | |
|---|---|---|---|
| Model | Chassis | Chassis & 3-Man Cab | Dropside & 3-Man Cab |
| 11' 10" wheelbase | £250 | £280 | £310 |
| 13' 10" wheelbase | £265 | £295 | £330 |
| All Prices Ex Depot, London. | | | |

*The heart of a truck is its engine; even as the human heart is the creator of energy, so the engine of a truck transmits its power in order to achieve a purpose.*

*The sinews of the OPEL TRUCK are mighty ones. 5 Speeds forward and one reverse (4th and 5th silent), gears helically cut, transform that engine power into action.*

The 4-bearing crankshaft harmonically balanced, the exceptionally strong rear axle, the hydraulic brakes with 373 square inches braking surface ensure that action will be sure, safe and economical. The maximum torque of 175.1 foot lbs. permits the transmission of an unusually high percentage of the engine power at low engine speeds. The rear springs are mounted on the cross members and the wheel mountings are equipped with a special safety device to prevent the effects of loosened wheel bolts. The OPEL TRUCK classes as Under 50 Cwt., and there are ample modern comfort features for the driver, including a 3-man all-steel cab, no draught ventilation, safety glass all round, compartment in dash, large instrument board with passenger-car type instruments, and trafficators.

**VRITE** for catalogue and address of your nearest OPEL TRUCK dealer to: General Motors Ltd. (Dept. O.L. 10 ) , St. James's Square, London, S.W.1, Phone: Whitehall 3737. Service Parts, Depot: Corney Road, Chiswick, W.4. hone for Service, Chiswick 2664. Phone for Parts, Chiswick, 1829.

**A PRODUCT OF GENERAL MOTORS**

This Opel advertisement appeared in British trade journals at the time of the Commercial Motor Show held at Earls Court, London, in November 1937. The engine and gearbox shown could readily be mistaken for a Bedford unit, and in fact, in one respect the latter's 28hp engine which was yet to appear in production at that date, followed suit in switching to the starter mounting on the left-hand side as shown. The chassis prices quoted were just £5 more than those being charged for the contemporary Bedford 3-ton WTH and WTL models. It is noteworthy that quite strong emphasis is placed on General Motors in the advertisement, and the addresses quoted are of premises of that concern in St James's Square, London S.W.1 and Corney Road, Chiswick, W.4. There is no mention of Adam Opel AG or its address in Germany. At that date, and indeed for most of the period of production, Bedford advertisements made no mention of the General Motors connection, Vauxhall and Bedford having built up a strong identity of their own, by inference British.

# 7 THE WAR YEARS

When the Second World War began on 3rd September 1939, Vauxhall Motors had clear ideas as to the contribution it could make, even though the Government of the day had left many matters concerning military vehicle production needs until the eleventh hour. In the event, quite apart from huge production of a whole range of vehicle types, all adapted to war needs, Bedford was to find itself designing a new four-wheel-drive model and a 350bhp tank engine, both at short notice, taking over manufacture of the complete tank and many other items. It was also to suffer air raid damage, twice, and on the worst occasion, 30th August 1940, some 39 Vauxhall employees were killed.

Dealing first with military vehicles developed from normal Bedford products, the company had been developing a 15-cwt truck for military use since Bedford vehicles first participated in the Army trials of 1935, as mentioned in Chapter Five. The method used by the War Department when inviting participation by manufacturers in its contracts was to issue a specification laying down the main requirements for the type of vehicle required and then the manufacturers would submit designs meeting those requirements. In some cases, they would be for completely specialised vehicles, but in others manufacturers were encouraged, in order to allow rapid and economic production, to incorporate standard units or even base the designs on standard models as supplied to civilian users, modified in regard to such items as tyre equipment, increased ground clearance, springs, modified cooling and air cleaners, towing facilities etc.

Thus this specification called for a 15-cwt truck, 4 x 2, G.S. The 4 x 2 referred to the total number of axles and the number driven and G.S. signified General Service.

Several makers submitted designs and in due course obtained contracts, though the Bedford was probably the best known. Becoming known as type MW, it was comparable to a 30-cwt model in general design, save for the broad bonnet with sloping top. That feature had begun as a means of incorporating military specification features, notably a very bulky air cleaner specified on some military vehicles. This was not adopted for production, but the military authorities still insisted that the sloping bonnet be kept, apparently related to ease of decontamination in the event of gas attack, which preoccupied those planning for the foreseen threats of what was described as 'total war'. Hence it extended to all bonneted Bedfords to military specification. In a curious way, it gave a clue to design trends of later years, with the headlamps incorporated in the front panel, though it was strictly utilitarian in concept.

The military models also had a sturdy 'crash bar' across the radiator, protecting it from damage in a minor collision.

What was also noteworthy is that the semi-forward-control 'short-bonnet' layout was specified on military 15-cwt and 30-cwt models, and not just confined to the 3-ton (or 5-ton) category as applied in the civilian range, although the dimensions of all three types were rather disguised by the military front-end.

The MW had a very short, 99in (8ft 3in), wheelbase and had large-section tyres on small, 16-in diameter, wheels, the actual size being 9.00 x 16. Having the standard 27.34hp six-cylinder engine of 3.5-litre capacity in so compact a vehicle made it very lively, and the illusion of quite a powerful sports car was increased by the aero screens and open cab of the original design. It was by no means unknown for these vehicles to be driven by young Army drivers, both officers and other ranks, as if they *were* sports cars, and with relatively modest weight and quite a low centre of gravity, they handled quite well in addition to having very lively acceleration.

However, more seriously, they were intended to provide rugged yet nimble transport, and it was realised that these, and other types, would be needed in large numbers in time of war as the Army, Royal Navy and Royal Air Force expanded. The more specialised types built in much more limited numbers largely by much smaller concerns such as Guy, Thornycroft and Crossley for the peacetime Army could not be made available in the quantities needed from such sources, or even from the larger heavy commercial vehicle makers, whose output would be needed for other products to which their facilities were suited.

In this context, it is significant that a meeting had been held in November 1938, when Vauxhall Motors had been approached about designing and developing a four-wheel-drive (4 x 4) truck, which again would probably be needed in quantity. On 2nd May, 1939, a further meeting was held at Luton between Government officials and senior members of the company. Possible production figures were discussed relating to the 15-cwt truck, and small-scale production of this type authorised. Manufacture of larger models in the 30-cwt and 3-ton classes was also discussed, and there was also further talk on the 4 x 4, although no firm decisions on this were taken.

When war came, output of the first deliveries of 15-cwt MW models was in hand, examples going to all three services as well as Government departments, though the Army was the main recipient. Output of the new civilian K, M and O ranges had only been running for barely three months and the military authorities, faced with an immediate and large need for vehicles, specified that many of these, and in particular O-types, were to be impressed – in other words, compulsorily acquired.

Lined-up in a works compound ready for delivery are 52 of the early production MW 15-cwt Army trucks, together with various civilian O and M types. The absence of headlamp masks or white-edged mudguards on any of the latter or what were doubtless employees' cars parked in the roadway outside indicates that this scene almost certainly dates from shortly before war was declared on 3rd September, 1939 – the black-out regulations took effect immediately afterwards. Authorisation for an initial order for the MW model had been agreed on 2nd May 1939 and these vehicles were doubtless the first fruits of that step. They are of the early type with what was called a cape cart hood and aero-type windscreens, the latter of a style then associated with racing or sports cars, and Army drivers soon discovered that a lusty 3.5-litre six-cylinder engine in quite a small vehicle allowed the MW to be driven in an appropriately sporting manner.

It is very probable that most of the shiny new civilian Bedfords, looking very smart with their new-style cabs, were requisitioned for military use, as occurred on quite a large scale in the early weeks of the war. Note how many bicycles are parked against the wall on the other side of the roadway. In those days, this would be a major means of transport for employees – the cars, mainly Ford Eight or elderly Morris types, were probably owned by foremen, this being before the days when it was normal for car factory workers to purchase the products of their employers. There seems no formal arrangement for parking either cars or bikes, doubtless owned by workers in the nearby workshops, implying that others would be similarly dotted around the factory.

An early example of the MW fitted with a 22mm gun, the mounting of which was designed by Vauxhall Motors. The recoil effect must have caused the vehicle to jump around quite considerably on those low-pressure tyres. This variant was much less common than the G.S. truck. This view shows how this military model has the semi-forward-control layout, with prominent engine cowl alongside the steering column, of the civilian 3- and 5-ton models although derived from the 2-ton model in mechanical features. The aeroscreen idea was appealing in good weather but the type became nicknamed 'the pneumonia wagon' by the men and women who drove them, especially in the very severe weather of the first winter of the war.

My colleague Alan Townsin, newly in Penrith, Cumberland, as a 13-year-old schoolboy evacuee, has a vivid recollection of a convoy of them, at that stage still gleaming in the not-long-painted various bright liveries of their erstwhile civilian owners, drawn up by the roadside of the A6 main road from Scotland in the town centre while their Army drivers stopped for a breather on their way south. Somehow it conveyed, more vividly than anything he had seen, how normal life was going to be disrupted by the war. The vehicles taken were generally those with standard dropside or sometimes tipper bodies and, after repainting in the gloomy matt khaki, no doubt many of them went with the British Expeditionary Force to France, only to be lost the following summer when the Dunkirk evacuation meant that vehicles had to be left behind — many were driven into the harbour or otherwise destroyed to prevent them falling into enemy hands. During the rest of the war, seeing a new-style civilian Bedford to the 1939 vee-screen cab specification would be a rare event, most of the survivors being those with special bodies which were of no interest to the military.

Production of Vauxhall cars and civilian-type Bedford trucks continued for a few months but on a limited scale, many of them being for Government or other war-related users. Before long, however, the production lines were busy with military vehicles, being turned out at a rate of almost a thousand a week and that was to continue to be so until 1945 despite Vauxhall also being involved with many other contributions to the war effort.

Soon, the MW 15-cwt was joined by the OX 30-cwt model with 111in (9ft 3in) wheelbase, fitted with 10.50x16 tyres apart from early examples on the more conventional 34x7 size, and the most familiar of all wartime types, the OY 3-tonner with 157in (13ft 1in) wheelbase, also mostly on 10.50x16 tyres, using singles at the rear, apart from early examples which had civilian-style smaller 32x6 tyres on twin rear wheels.

All these military vehicles had 12-volt electrical equipment and, unusually among Bedford vehicles, Solex carburettors; civilian Bedfords of virtually all models used Zenith carburettors of various types. The adoption of large single rear tyres was to give better capability of running

A dockside scene as an MW 15-cwt G.S. truck is swung aloft and a row of OYD 3-tonners stands on railway wagons. This scene almost certainly dates from autumn 1939 as the vessel, evidently a conventional freighter, is still in peacetime colours. Wartime camouflage was very soon adopted for all ships, civilian as well as military, to make them less vulnerable to air or submarine attack. The style of railway wagon suggests that this photograph may have been taken in France, as part of the British Expeditionary Force arrived to support the French army in defending that country against German attack. Further 15-cwt trucks are parked in the foreground together with some Bren gun carriers, the latter being very light tracked vehicles powered by Ford V8 engines. Note that the OYD models have conventional civilian wheels and tyres, with twins at the rear – this equipment was used for the early military 3-tonners but quite soon abandoned in favour of the style of wheel with much larger tyres as used on the MW. The broad tyres proved much better at coping with soft ground or sand, and gave British vehicles an advantage compared to the Germans, for the typical military Opel continued to have twin tyres through the war.

Modest numbers of Bedford vehicles to basically civilian design were built for military use, such as this 30-cwt model for the Royal Air Force. The normal style of grille and bonnet are retained, though the bonnet sides have additional cooling grilles whose history may well go back to the pre-war War Department trials when cooling performance on a severe climb was judged below par even though the manufacturer's own engineers did not consider it so. The dropside body with canvas tilt top was, and still is, much favoured by the military. Note the civilian-style tail lamp, complete with chromium-plated finish, a design inherited from the Chevrolet of 1929.

over soft or uneven ground, the tyres having deep coarse treads which added their own sound to the familiar Bedford mixture of throaty engine note and wailing gearbox – the different bonnet also appeared to alter the engine note somewhat, possibly because of the fitting of larger fans in at least some cases to cope with tropical conditions.

The OX and OY series had the 1939-style cab, with divided vee windscreen, its stylish curves now seeming ill-at-ease in dingy-looking khaki and behind the utilitarian bonnet, with an abrupt change of direction from the latter's slope to the horizontal waistline which formed part of the cab pressings. After a while, some of these cabs were supplied with a mounting ring in the nearside roof to allow fitting of a machine gun as a defence against air attack.

Quite a variety of bodywork was fitted on these three main military types; the most familiar was the G. S. lorry with canvas cover or tilt, the full Bedford designations for these being MWD, OXD and OYD. The 3-ton OYD in

particular was the most common full-sized British Army lorry of the Second World War, and indeed remained such for many years afterwards. The chassis number series appear to indicate that 72,385 OY models were built, most of them OYD, plus 65,995 of the 15-cwt MW and 24,429 of the OX, but the sub-divisions were complex and in some ways quite different from those applying in peacetime. Even so, the OY total alone is comparable to that of the nation's entire bus and coach fleet, so it is no wonder the pre-war Bedford motto 'You see them everywhere' still applied in wartime.

In particular, the OX designation included the OXC, mainly used to haul semi-trailers and corresponding to the equivalent civilian 3-ton models, some with twin rear tyres and others with the military-style fat singles. Many of these were Bedford-Scammell outfits, with the automatic coupling arrangement as introduced in civilian form in 1939, though others had semi-trailers of various types, largely made by

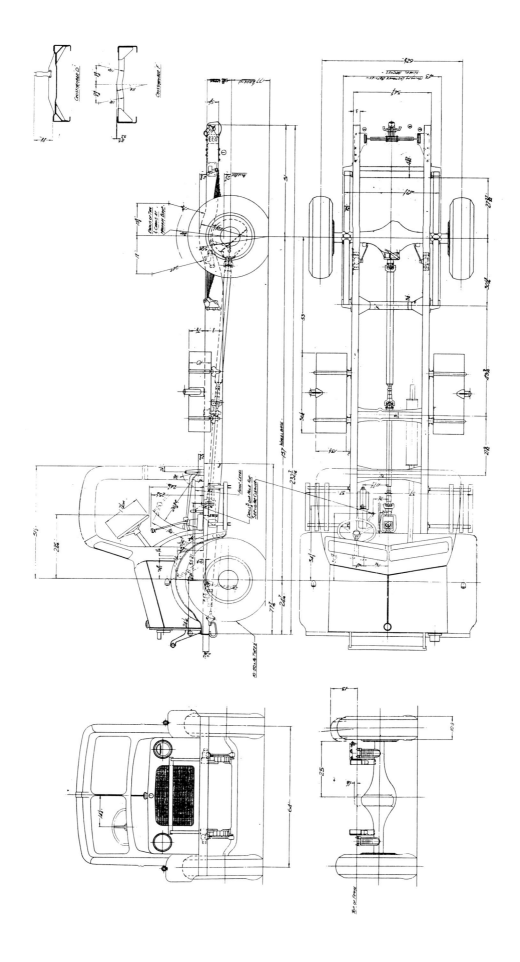

This Vauxhall Motors engineering department drawing shows the OY 3-ton chassis in its most usual form with 10.50x16 tyres. It conveys how uneasily the wartime style of bonnet and the curves of the pressed steel cab married together, the lines not merging smoothly in elevation, plan or front view. Yet this was typical of wartime, when matters which would have been regarded as important in normal circumstances were brushed aside under the imperatives of the times. The original drawing dated from December 1939, no doubt soon after the decision to standardize on this tyre size had been made. Note that only one masked headlamp was provided, the space for the offside one often being occupied by a plate identifying the unit to which the vehicle belonged. The twin fuel tanks were mounted higher than on civilian models to ensure that they would not be damaged when negotiating uneven ground.

The OXC tractor was used with a Taskers low loading semi-trailer by the RAF as an aircraft transporter, moving aircraft where it was impractical to fly them, including the recovery of those which had made forced landings or crashed as well as to or from workshops with no take-off or landing facilities nearby. The smaller aircraft could be carried complete or nearly so, but with wings and tail removed, as in the case of this Spitfire lacking propeller, or the cowling over its Rolls-Royce Merlin engine. Note the AEC Matador 4x4, another classic military vehicle of the war years, on the right.

Tasker of Andover, one of the leading makers of large trailers and semi-trailers.

Apart from the G.S. trucks and lorries – at that stage, the distinction seems to have been that 'truck' applied to the 15cwt whereas the description for the 30-cwt and 3-ton versions was 'lorry' – there was a remarkable variety of body types built. There were water tankers on the 15-cwt, classified MWC; a gun-mounting version, MWG; a wireless vehicle, MWR; an anti-tank gun tractor, MWT and a van, MWV. The early version with open cab and aero screens later gave way to one with a more substantial windscreen and metal doors to waist height, but even the latter, described as a 'closed cab', had a canvas top with side screens.

Of the OX types, the standard rigid version was the OXD lorry with tilt, but the OXC tractive unit with semi-trailers had a wide variety of bodywork including platform or dropside but also petrol tankers of 1,200 or 2,000 gallon capacity, with tanks by the Steel Barrel Co, the larger being a Bedford-Scammell.

The RAF used some OXC models with a special type of low-loading long Tasker semi-trailer with an internal length of 34ft for carrying aircraft, nicknamed 'Queen Marys' after the famous liner which was almost the largest ship in the world at the time. They were big enough to carry a complete fighter with wings removed and placed alongside the fuselage, or could take sections of larger aircraft. Among their duties was the recovery of damaged aircraft, and the type was a common sight on the roads of Britain in those years. As with most military types, various suppliers made other versions of this type and, in this country at least, the Bedford in this aircraft-carrying role was rather less common than a Commer or Crossley equivalent. The Navy used another version specially adapted to the carrying of torpedoes.

An odd-looking variant of the OY was the OYC petrol tanker version, in which the modest-sized 800-gallon tank was quite low-built and covered by a canvas tilt top, making it less conspicuous to enemy aircraft when among a convoy of lorries of similar general appearance. There were also water-carrying versions.

(continued on page 106

Later MW models had what was euphemistically called a closed cab, as here, despite the fact that it still had a hood and sidescreens. However it did have a full-width windscreen and side doors, though they are unlikely to have prevented this driver getting his feet wet. It appears that a test was being carried out in a boating lake, watched by an appreciative crowd of 'squaddies' plus what were probably Ministry men, as well as the odd schoolboy. The objective was to find out if basically standard vehicles could be made to negotiate water of this depth, say when climbing on to beaches from landing craft, in preparation for the invasion of Europe. The canvas screen over the radiator may have been an attempt to prevent an excessive bow wave. It seems certain that some work had been done to seal the ignition system as the distributor must have been below water level. Clearly forward progress was being made, as the driver looks remarkably happy in the circumstances.

It is sometimes said that the British fought the war on cups of tea. In general the MW was not a 'civilian' model, but some were used for purposes such as this – the phrase 'tea car' has a delightful ring to it. The Young Men's Christian Association, better known by the initials YMCA, played a major part in looking after the social needs of serving soldiers, sailors and airmen. The purpose of such vehicles was to be able to reach troops even if rough ground had to be negotiated and they were much appreciated in places like remote anti-aircraft batteries as well as busy camps, airfields or dockyards.

In January 1944, Vauxhall Motors Ltd issued a remarkable booklet giving visual identification and brief specifications of Bedford vehicles and Vauxhall cars supplied to Government contracts or released for approved civilian use by the Ministry of War Transport. It was marked 'Not to be published', being evidently intended for military transport officers etc. The following pages are reproduced from it. The sheer variety of wartime production is conveyed though, no doubt deliberately, no details of quantities were included, some of the types shown being very rare. Clearly a very competent artist was used, even if working from photographs, and although a utilitarian document, the pages now have quite an artistic appeal.

| Illus-tration No. | Model | Description | Tyres | Wheel-base | Engine Bore and Stroke in millimetres | Body | Interior Dimensions Length x Width x Height |
|---|---|---|---|---|---|---|---|
| 1 | MWC | Bedford 15-cwt., 4 x 2, Water Tanker | 9.00 x 16 (Single Rear) | 99" | W.D. Type 6 cyl: 27.34 h.p. 85.72 x 101.6 | Cape Cart Hood. 230 Gallon Tank Pumps & Equipment (Thompson Bros.) | — |
| | | (Note : Later vehicles have closed cab as illustration 2). | | | | | |
| 2 | MWD | Bedford 15-cwt. 4 x 2, G.S. Truck | 9.00 x 16 (Single Rear) | 99" | W.D. Type 6 cyl: 27.34 h.p. 85.72 x 101.6 | Canvas Hood. Lorry Body (now with Tilt) | 77½" x 70¼" x 54" |
| | | (Note : Early vehicles have open cab as illustration 1 and flat canvas cover over body). | | | | | |
| | MWG | Bedford 15-cwt., 4 x 2, G.S. Truck with Gun Mountings | 9.00 x 16 (Single Rear) | 99" | W.D. Type 6 cyl: 27.34 h.p. 85.72 x 101.6 | Cape Cart Hood. Lorry Body with Gun Mounting and Seats | 77½" x 70¼" x 22" |
| | | (Note : Supplied with open cab, and ditching boards on the outside of the body sides). | | | | | |
| 3 | MWR | Bedford 15-cwt., 4 x 2, Fitted for Wireless | 9.00 x 16 (Single Rear) | 99" | W.D. Type 6 cyl: 27.34 h.p. 85.72 x 101.6 | Canvas Hood. Wireless Vehicle. Signals Body | 77½" x 70¼" x 55" |
| 4 | MWT | Bedford 15-cwt., 4 x 2, Anti-Tank Tractor | 9.00 x 16 (Single Rear) | 99" | W.D. Type 6 cyl: 27.34 h.p. 85.72 x 101.6 | Cape Cart Hood. Lorry Body with Seats, Tilt and Drawbar | 77½" x 70¼" x 54" |
| | | (Note : Body sides as illustration 2, and tilt with windows). | | | | | |
| | MWV | Bedford 15-cwt., 4 x 2, G.S. Van | 9.00 x 16 Cross Ctry. (Single Rear) | 99" | W.D. Type 6 cyl: 27.34 h.p. 85.72 x 101.6 | Cape Cart Hood. Lorry Body with Tilt | 90" x 72" x 54" |
| | | (Note : Later vehicles have closed cab as illustration 2). | | | | | |
| 5 | OXD | Bedford 30-cwt., 4 x 2, G.S. Lorry | Were 34×7, now 10.50 x 16 (Single Rear) | 111" | W.D. Type 6 cyl: 27.34 h.p. 85.72 x 101.6 | Standard Steel Cab. Lorry Body with Tilt | 104" x 78" x 66" |
| 6 | OXC | Bedford-Scammell, 6-ton, 4 x 2 — 2, Semi-Trailer Lorry | 32 x 6 (Dual Rear) | 274" (Combined) | W.D. Type 6 cyl: 27.34 h.p. 85.72 x 101.6 | Standard Steel Cab. Lorry Body (Scammell) | 240" x 84" x 36" |
| 7 | OXC | Bedford-Scammell, 6-ton, 4 x 2 — 2, Semi-Trailer Flat Platform Lorry | Were 32×6 (Dual Rear) now 10.50×16 (Single Rear) | 218" (Combined) | W.D. Type 6 cyl: 27.34 h.p. 85.72 x 101.6 | Standard Steel Cab. Flat Platform (Scammell) | 180" x 84" |
| 8 | OXC | Bedford 30-cwt., 4 x 2, Mobile Canteen | 10.50 x 16 (Single Rear) | 111" | W.D. Type 6 cyl: 27.34 h.p. 85.72 x 101.6 | Standard Steel Cab. Body (Spurling) | 102" x 72" x 69½" |
| 9 | OXC | Bedford-Scammell, 4 x 2 — 2, Semi-Trailer Petrol Tanker | 32 x 6 (Dual Rear) | 274" (Combined) | W.D. Type 6 cyl: 27.34 h.p. 85.72 x 101.6 | Standard Steel Cab. 2,000 Gallon, 3-Compartment Petrol Tank (Steel Barrel Co.) | — |

| Illustration No. | Model | Description | Tyres | Wheelbase | Engine Bore and Stroke in millimetres | Body | Interior Dimensions Length x Width x Height |
|---|---|---|---|---|---|---|---|
| **10** | OXC | Bedford-Scammell, 6-ton, 4 x 2 — 2, Semi-Trailer Dropside Lorry | 32 x 6 (Dual Rear) | 258" (Combined) | W.D. Type 6 cyl: 27.34 h.p. 85.72 x 101.6 | Standard Steel Cab. Dropside Lorry Body (Scammell) | 237" x 84" x 18" |
| **11** | OXC | Bedford-Scammell, 4 x 2 — 2, Semi-Trailer Petrol Tanker | 32 x 6 (Dual Rear) | 231" (Combined) | W.D. Type 6 cyl: 27.34 h.p. 85.72 x 101.6 | Standard Steel Cab. 1,200 gall., 3-Compartment Petrol Tank (Steel Barrel) | — |
| **12** | OXC | Bedford Tractor, 3-ton, 4 x 2 — 2, Semi-Trailer (Tasker) | Tractor 10.50 x 16 Trailer 10.50 x 20 (Singles) | 407½" (Combined) | W.D. Type 6 cyl: 27.34 h.p. 85.72 x 101.6 | Standard Steel Cab. High Loading Trailer (Taskers) | 398" x 86¼" x 2⅞" |
| **13** | OXC | Bedford Tractor, 4 x 2 — 2, Semi-Trailer Bus. (R. A. Dyson and British Trailer Co.) | 32 x 6 (Dual Rear) | 285" (Combined) | W.D. Type 6 cyl: 27.34 h.p. 85.72 x 101.6 | Standard Steel Cab. Body (C. H, Roe) "Bevin Bus" | 295" x 97" x 80‑9⁄16" Carrying Capacity—65 |
| **14** | OXC | Bedford Tractor, 3-ton, 4 x 2 — 2, Semi-Trailer (Tasker) (*Note* : Also 5-ton, 4 x 2—2, as above, except semi-trailer fitted with 13.50 x 20 tyres.) | Tractor 10.50 x 16 Trailer 10.50 x 20 | 446½" (Combined) | W.D. Type 6 cyl: 27.34 h.p. 85.72 x 101.6 | Standard Steel Cab. Low Loading Trailer (Taskers) | 408" x 72" x 30" |
| **15** | OXC | Bedford Tractor, 4 x 2 — 4, Semi-Trailer (Trailer Appliance) | Tractor 10.50 x 16 Trailer 10.50 x 20 (now 4 singles in line) | 363" (Combined) | W.D. Type 6 cyl: 27.34 h.p. 85.72 x 101.6 | Standard Steel Cab. Torpedo-Carrying Attachment | — |
| **16** | OYC | Bedford, 3-ton, 4 x 2, Petrol Tanker (*Note* : Also Water Tanker as above, 350 gall. and 500 gall. tank—Butterfields.) | 10.50 x 16 (Single Rear) | 157" | W.D. Type 6 cyl: 27.34 h.p. 85.72 x 101.6 | Standard Steel Cab. 800 gall., 2-Cpt. Petrol Tank (Steel Barrel Co.) | — |
| **17** | OYD | Bedford 3-ton, 4 x 2, G.S. Lorry | Were 32 x 6 Heavy Duty (Dual Rear) now 10.50 x 16 (Single Rear) | 157" | W.D. Type 6 cyl: 27.34 h.p. 85.72 x 101.6 | Standard Steel Cab. Lorry Body with Tilt | 138" x 78" x 72" |
| **18** | QLB | Bedford 3-ton, Tractor, 4 x 4, Light A.A. | 10.50 x 20 (Single Rear) | 143" | W.D. Type 6 cyl: 27.34 h.p. 85.72 x 101.6 | Standard Steel Cab. Bofors Gun Tractor | Crew Compartment 51" x 82¾" x 55" |

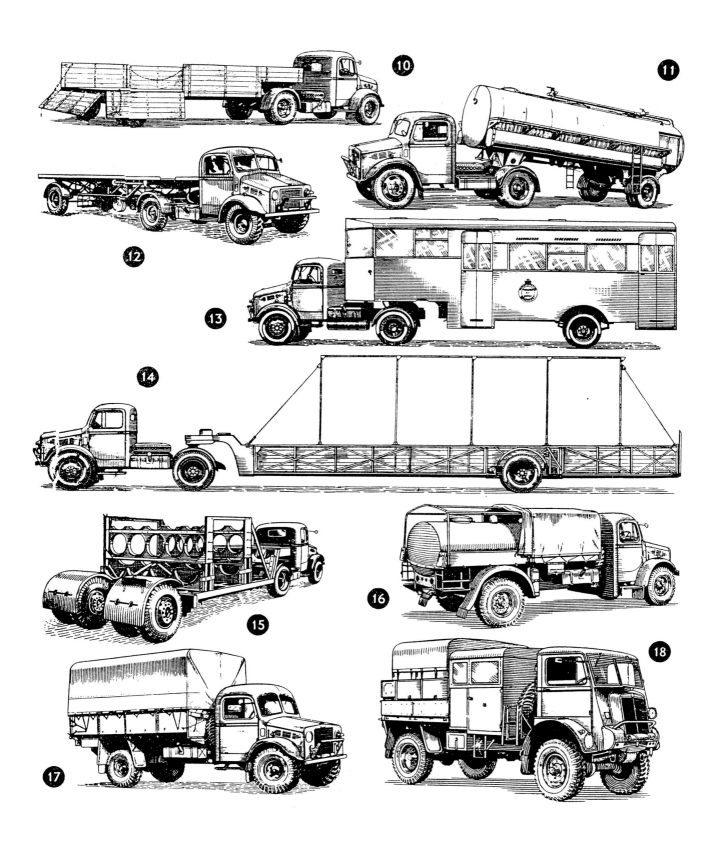

| Illus-tration No. | Model | Description | Tyres | Wheel-base | Engine Bore and Stroke in millimetres | Body | Interior Dimensions Length x Width x Height |
|---|---|---|---|---|---|---|---|
| ⑲ | QLC | Bedford 3-ton, 4 x 4, Petrol Tanker | 10.50 x 20 (Single Rear) | 143″ | W.D. Type 6 cyl: 27.34 h.p. 85.72 x 101.6 | Standard Steel Cab. 1,000 gall. Petrol Tank (Butterfields) | — |
| | | | *(Note : Tank now 950 gallons capacity.)* | | | | |
| ⑳ | QLD | Bedford 3-ton, 4 x 4, Lorry | 10.50 x 20 (Single Rear) | 143″ | W.D. Type 6 cyl: 27.34 h.p. 85.72 x 101.6 | Standard Steel Cab. Lorry Body with Tilt | 150¾″ x 83⅞″ x 72″ |
| ㉑ | QLT | Bedford 3-ton, 4 x 4, Troop Carrying | 10.50 x 20 (Single Rear) | 143″ | W.D. Type 6 cyl: 27.34 h.p. 85.72 x 101.6 | Standard Steel Cab. Troop Carrier Body with Tilt | 190″ x 85½″ x 72″ Seating Capacity—30 (plus Driver) |
| ㉒ | QLR | Bedford 3-ton, 4 x 4, Fitted for Wireless | 10.50 x 20 (Single Rear) | 143″ | W.D. Type 6 cyl: 27.34 h.p. 85.72 x 101.6 | Standard Steel Cab. Wireless Vehicle. Signals Body | 152″ x 80″ x 63″ |
| | | | *(Note : Also used as Command or Cypher vehicle.)* | | | | |
| ㉓ | QLC | Bedford Tractor, 6-ton, 4 x 4—2, Semi-Trailer (Glover, Webb & Liversedge) | 10.50 x 20 | 303″ | W.D. Type 6 cyl: 27.34 h.p. 85.72 x 101.6 | Standard Steel Cab. Body by Glover, Webb & Liversedge & S.M.T. | 203″ x 79″ x 30″ |
| ㉔ | OWST | Bedford 5-ton short wheelbase Tipper (Civilian Model to MOWT Licence) | 32 x 6 Front 34 x 7 Twin Rear | 111″ | 6 cyl: 27.34 h.p. 85.72 x 101.6 | Standard Steel Cab. Tipping Body | 97½″ x 78¼″ x 25″ |
| ㉕ | OWLE | Bedford 5-ton long wheelbase Flat Platform Lorry (Civilian Model to MOWT Licence) | 32 x 6 Front 34 x 7 Twin Rear | 157″ | 6 cyl: 27.34 h.p. 85.72 x 101.6 | Standard Steel Cab. Platform Body | 169½″ x 78″ |
| ㉖ | OWLD | Bedford 5-ton long wheelbase Dropside Truck (Civilian Model to MOWT Licence) | 32 x 6 Front 34 x 7 Twin Rear | 157″ | 6 cyl: 27.34 h.p. 85.72 x 101.6 | Standard Steel Cab. Dropside Body | 169″ x 78″ x 17¾″ |
| ㉗ | OWB | Bedford 32-seater Bus (Civilian Model to MOWT Licence) | 7.50 x 20 Front 8.25 x 20 Twin Rear | 174″ | 6 cyl: 27.34 h.p. 85.72 x 101.6 | Bus Body (Duple) | 245″ x 80¾″ x 73¼″ |

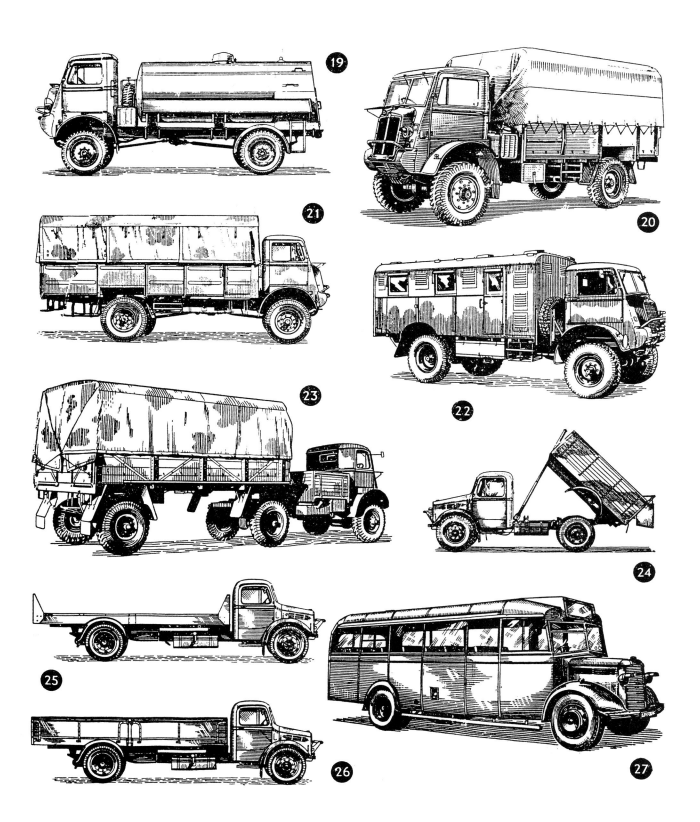

| Model | Description | Tyres | Wheel-base | Engine Bore and Stroke in m/m. | Body | Interior Dimensions Length x Width x Height | Visual Identification |
|-------|-------------|-------|-----------|-------------------------------|------|--------------------------------------------|----------------------|
| BYC | Bedford 12-cwt. Utility Van | 5.50 x 17 (Single Rear) | 106½" | 6 cyl: 19.8 h.p. 73 x 95.25 | Utility Body (Greenhous) 2 collapsible seats | 73" x 59" x 51" | |
| JCV | Bedford 10/12-cwt. "Utilecon" | 5.25 x 17 (Single Rear) | 105" | 4 cyl: 12 h.p. 69.5 x 95 | Utilecon Body (Martin Walter) 7 collapsible seats. Convertible Van | 78" x 53" x 42" | |
| JCV | Bedford 10/12-cwt. Van | 5.25 x 17 (Single Rear) | 105" | 4 cyl: 12 h.p. 69.5 x 95 | Hardwood and Steel ; double doors | 78" x 53" x 47" | |
| K | Bedford 30/40-cwt. Lorry | 32 x 6 Truck type (Single Rear) | 120" | 6 cyl: 27.34 h.p. 85.72 x 101.6 | Standard Steel Cab. Lorry with Tilt | 97½" x 66½" x 72" | |
| MSC | Bedford 30-cwt. Tender | 10.50 x 16 (Single Rear) | 120" | 6 cyl: 27.34 h.p. 85.72 x 101.6 | Standard Steel Cab. Lorry with Tilt (Spurling) | 116" x 72" x 72" | |
| MS | Bedford 2/3-ton 3-way Tipper | 32 x 6 Truck type (Dual Rear) | 120" | 6 cyl: 27.34 h.p. 85.72 x 101.6 | Standard Steel Cab. Body and Hydraulic Gear (Bromilow and Edwards) | 97" x 78" x 18" | |
| MS | Bedford 2/3-ton End Tipper | 32 x 6 Truck type (Dual Rear) | 120" | 6 cyl: 27.34 h.p. 85.72 x 101.6 | Standard Steel Cab. Body (Spurling), Hand-Operating Gear (Spenborough) | 97" x 73" x 18" | |
| ML | Bedford 2/3-ton Lorry | 32 x 6 Heavy Duty (Dual Rear) | 143" | 6 cyl: 27.34 h.p. 85.72 x 101.6 | Standard Steel Cab. Lorry with Tilt | 138" x 73" x 18" | |
| ML Modified | Bedford Petrol Tanker | 32 x 6 Heavy Duty (Dual Rear) | 143" | 6 cyl: 27.34 h.p. 85.72 x 101.6 | Standard Steel Cab. 800 gallon 4-Compartment Tank (Aluminium Plant & Vessel Co.) | — | |

| Model | Description | Tyres | Wheel-base | Engine Bore and Stroke in m/m. | Body | Interior Dimensions Length x Width x Height | Visual Identification |
|---|---|---|---|---|---|---|---|
| ML Modi-fied | Bedford Ambulance | 10.50 x 16 (Single Rear) | 143" | 6 cyl: 27.34 h.p. 85.72 x 101.6 | 4-Stretcher Ambulance Body (Mann Egerton) | — | |
| ML Modi-fied | Bedford 2/3-ton End Tipper | Front 7.00 x 20 Single Rear & Spare 7.00 x 34 | 143" | 6 cyl: 27.34 h.p. 85.72 x 101.6 | Standard Steel Cab. Body (Spurling), Hand Operating Gear (Clayton Dewandre) | 126" x 78" x 18" | |
| OS | Bedford 3/4-ton 3-Way Tipper | 32 x 6 Heavy Duty (Dual Rear) | 111" | 6 cyl: 27.34 h.p. 85.72 x 101.6 | Standard Steel Cab. Body and Hydraulic Gear (Bromilow and Edwards) | 97" x 78" x 21" | |
| OL | Bedford 3/4-ton Lorry | 32 x 6 Heavy Duty (Dual Rear) | 157" | 6 cyl: 27.34 h.p. 85.72 x 101.6 | Standard Steel Cab. Lorry Body | 168" x 78" x 18" | |
| OS | Bedford-Scammell Tractor-Trailer Combination 6-Ton | 32 x 6 Heavy Duty (Dual Rear) | 274" | 6 cyl: 27.34 h.p. 85.72 x 101.6 | Standard Steel Cab. Lorry Body (Scammell) | 238" x 84" | |
| H | Vauxhall 4-Seater Saloon | 5.00 x 16 (Single Rear) | 94" | 4 cyl: 10 h.p. 63.5 x 95 | Standard Steel Saloon. Sliding Roof | Overall Length 155½" Overall Width 59¾" | |
| I | Vauxhall 4-Seater Saloon | 5.25 x 16 (Single Rear) | 104" | 4 cyl: 12 h.p. 69. 5 x 95 | Standard Steel Saloon. Sliding Roof | Overall Length 162¼" Overall Width 61¾" | |
| J | Vauxhall 5-Seater Saloon | 5.50 x 16 (Single Rear) | 105" | 6 cyl: 14.07 h.p. 61.5 x 100 | Standard Steel Saloon. Sliding Roof | Overall Length 168¼" Overall Width 64" | |
| GY | Vauxhall 5-Seater Saloon | 6.50 x 16 (Single Rear) | 111" | 6 cyl: 24.97 h.p. 81.94 x 101.6 | Standard Wood and Steel Saloon. Sliding Roof | Overall Length 184¼" Overall Width 71½" | |

The QL 4x4 was quite different from any Bedford that had gone before, not only because of its four-wheel drive but because of its full forward-control layout and its high build, the latter partly related to the space needed under the engine for the driven front axle but also to some degree deliberate to improve its capability in conditions such as this. The Bedfordshire trade plates and civilian driver indicate that this was a development vehicle, doubtless being tested to confirm that it was performing as intended. Following submission of a preliminary specification in October 1939, detailed design and construction of a prototype was completed a year later and production began early in 1941, continuing at about 12,000 per year until 1944, alongside even larger numbers of other models.

continued from page 96)

Apart from all the foregoing Bedford military vehicles recognisably derived from the pre-war civilian range, the 4x4 project that had been discussed at the pre-war meetings with Government representatives came to life. On 12th September 1939, nine days after the war began, there was a further meeting on the possibilities, though it was made clear that no firm decision had been reached. On the 26th, authorisation was given for ordering material to construct a prototype and on 12th October a preliminary specification was submitted by the engineering team. It was well received and approved as a basis for producing prototypes, which Vauxhall was asked to do as quickly as possible. On receipt of this, C. E. King, as Chief Engineer, circulated a memorandum dated 16th November, saying 'No work of any description whatsoever is to be allowed to interfere with the carrying out of all work necessary in the development of the 4x4 vehicle.'

Because of its four-wheel-drive, the QL, as it was to become known, was considerably higher-built than previous Bedford models, the drive to both front and rear axles being taken from a centrally-mounted transfer gearbox. The drive to the front axle thus passed forward below the engine and there had to be sufficient clearance under the sump for the bulky differential casing in the centre of the front axle. It was also decided to adopt forward-control layout, for the first time in a Bedford, except for a very limited number of conversions to this layout made by other concerns in pre-war days. On this model single wheels with large-section tyres were again used and as these were 10.50x20 size of larger diameter than the type used on the OY etc, this again increased the vehicle's height. This high build also had a practical advantage that was to become very important later in the war, since it made the QL better able to land on beachheads from landing craft and negotiate streams or

# Q.L.  BEDFORD CHASSIS

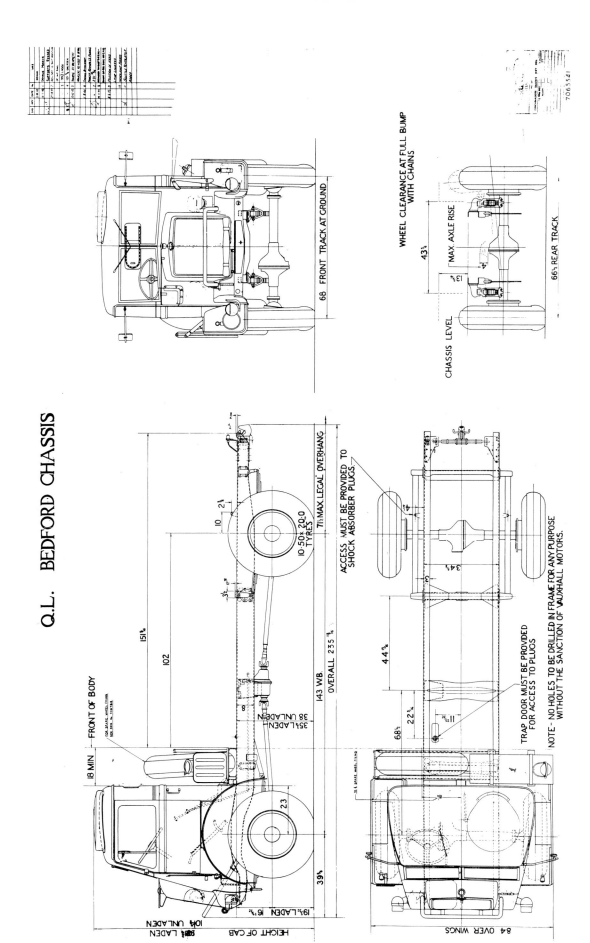

This general arrangement drawing of the QL chassis with standard cab conveys its high build. Note the massive but crude mechanically-operated semaphore-type direction indicator fitted on the left side only, the driver being expected to make a hand signal if turning right.

The QL proved its worth in the North African campaign in 1942-43, where its sure-footed grip in sand was invaluable. The desert camouflage was quite a light sandy yellow colour and the informality of 'the desert war' is reflected in the names of wives or girl-friends attached to the radiator grille – one wonders if 'Betty', 'Joyce' and 'Dulcie' lived happily ever after with their menfolk.

flooded ground. The wheelbase was 143in (11ft 11in), which was 14in shorter than an OY but the internal length of the standard lorry body was longer, at 150¾in, than the OY's 138in, due to the more compact forward-control layout. A spare wheel was mounted behind the cab in both cases.

In consequence, the QL looked very different from any previous Bedford. A factory-made steel cab was fitted, and for this model a less-rounded design was adopted than used for the O-series, having a sloping front panel with a relatively conventional-looking radiator outline projecting forward – the rear part of the cab was not unlike the civilian type used in the 1934-38 period.

As some of the type were to haul guns and all were intended specifically for use over rough country, Bedford engineers would have liked to fit a larger engine, to provide more power but the military decided that standardisation of the power unit with that used so widely in other Bedford models was essential, hence the familiar 27.34hp unit was adopted. There was the four-speed main gearbox and the transfer gearbox, the latter seemingly the culprit for the high-pitched scream which accompanied the progress of the QL almost as soon as it got under way and was evident regardless of which gear was engaged, including top. However, little attention was paid to such matters under the pressures of wartime, even though no doubt the enemy would have been able to pick up the sound of a convoy of QLs from quite some distance.

The design work and construction of a prototype was carried out with the speed for which CEK had asked, and

By far the most numerous wartime Bedford was the OY, especially in this OYD form with standard tilt body. It became the British Army's standard general duty lorry and remained so for quite a number of years after the war was over. A measure of the total number of OY models built during the war years, 72,385 as indicated by the chassis numbers issued, is that they are roughly equivalent to the nation's entire present-day stock of buses used for carrying the public, from double-deckers down to minibuses.

the first experimental vehicle was undergoing trials by 1st October 1940, and the second and third prototypes were under way. They successfully completed trials carried out by the Army and at the same time, special tools and equipment for volume production were brought in. By March 1941 the first QLs were in production and to everyone's relief, the new model proved trouble-free despite the short gestation period.

After about twelve months of production, reports filtered back to the service department of brake judder which occurred only on a minority of vehicles when the brakes were lightly applied. The problem was eventually traced to certain batches of tyre with a deeply grooved tread. When tyres with a more normal tread were fitted the problem disappeared and it was decided to take no further action.

From 1941, the majority of medium-weight 4 x 4 trucks purchased by the British armed forces were manufactured by Bedford, the wartime output of QL models being around 12,000 per year during 1942-44. They began a tradition which was to continue in postwar years, with the RL of the 1950s and subsequent types, some of which are in service in Bosnia as this volume is being written.

The wartime QL models appeared in various roles, the QLB being the version used as a tractor for a Bofors light anti-aircraft gun. One version of the QLC was a petrol tanker with Butterfields tank of 1,000-gallon capacity, reduced slightly in later models to 950-gallon, though there was also a QLC articulated version, towing a Glover, Webb & Liversage semi-trailer with tilt cover. The QLD was the standard lorry with tilt and QLT was a troop-carrying version with longer body, the spare wheel mounting being taken out, and having seats for 30 soldiers. There was also a QLR wireless vehicle which could also be used as a command or cypher vehicle.

Among numerous purposes to which military Bedford models were put, the Haslar smoke generator was perhaps among the most unusual. Hundreds of the trailer-mounted units were used to produce smoke in an effort to hide cities threatened by German bomber raids on moonlit nights, though the effects were at best capricious depending on suitable wind speed and direction.

The engine for what became the Churchill tank was vastly bigger and more powerful than anything that had been produced by the Vauxhall works previously. Here the front views of the standard 28hp 3.5-litre Bedford six-cylinder unit and the 21-litre twelve-cylinder tank engine are shown at the same scale. The RAC rating of the latter worked out at 120hp, but it developed 350bhp as compared to the 72bhp of the truck engine. It was a 'flat twelve', with two banks of six cylinders, one each side of the crankshaft. Due to lack of space, Vauxhall engineers were forced to use a side valve layout when designing the engine for the Churchill tank.

## The Churchill tank

Meanwhile, Vauxhall Motors Ltd had found itself involved in the design and manufacture of a tank engine and then a complete tank, both areas completely new to it.

Referring to the desperate situation which had arisen in the summer of 1940, Winston Churchill subsequently said in Parliament "We had in the hands of the troops in the United Kingdom fewer than a hundred tanks. These, and those under production at the time, were of a type which had proved in battle in France to be too weak to stand up to the German tank guns...." At that point in the war, the German army had defeated all the armies it had encountered on the continent of Europe and an invasion of Britain seemed likely in a matter of months.

Over 500 British tanks had been sent to France in 1939-40, and although about 330,000 troops were brought back via Dunkirk, no tanks could be brought back via that route, and only 26 were recovered by other routes before France fell. Those in Britain at the end of this disastrous episode were, as Churchill had said, of types known to be inferior to their German counterparts.

Much earlier, the rapidity of the German advance into Poland in the early days of the war in September 1939, had begun to make it clear that a new British tank was also likely to be inadequate. This was the A20, then in process of being developed to a design laid down by the Mechanisation Board of the War Department and to be built by Harland and Wolff, the Belfast shipbuilders. However, it took some time for the implications to be realised fully and for action to correct them to be taken.

The design of the A20 was based largely on the principles of First World War tank warfare, when the battle lines had been relatively static. It was realised that it relied too much on such features as obstacle-crossing capability and armoured strength to withstand continued artillery bombardment and, in particular, was underpowered. It was agreed that a much more powerful engine than the 200bhp Meadows unit that had been selected was needed, and yet redesign of the tank hull to accommodate a physically bigger engine would have virtually meant starting again from scratch.

By the early months of 1940, Alex Taub had impressed the officials at the War Department with his grasp of engine design matters – his forthright words on the folly of thick engine oil in Army lorries during the severe winter that had just passed no doubt made an impression – and the problem was laid before him.

In essence it was to produce a 350bhp engine, to run on petrol, and to fit in the space available in the existing tank shell. Taub astonished everyone by claiming that he could build a prototype engine from scratch in 90 days. At the time, the largest engine – and virtually the only one – in production in the factory was the 27.34hp unit of 3.5-litre capacity, with an output of 72bhp in standard form.

Studies on the most effective layout and size of engine to meet the need were set up very quickly, and a 21-litre flat twelve-cylinder unit with side valves was decided upon. It was Alex Mitchell who came up with the side-valve layout and who was responsible for interpreting Taub's ideas on the new engine. He was a graduate of Glasgow University who had distinguished himself in mathematics, and was one of several engineers who had joined Vauxhall from Rolls-Royce, in this case in 1939.

This type of unit has six cylinders arranged horizontally on each side of a central crankshaft, and it was the restricted width available that led to a side-valve layout being adopted, for the only time on a Bedford engine, since this altered the proportions of the engine in such a way as to make it more compact. The major components were made in cast iron and it weighed 3,372lb.

In fact the engine was designed and built in 89 days under Taub's direction. It was started up for the first time on 11th June 1940, just days after the Dunkirk evacuation had involved the loss of most of Britain's existing stock of tanks, so the implications were immense. After a programme of testing and adjustments to obtain the optimum output, it gave the required 350bhp on the test bed on the 121st day, just over a month later. By that time, France had surrendered and effectively Britain stood alone.

Maurice Platt, another of Vauxhall's strong engineering team, having joined the company in 1937 from the editorial staff of *The Motor* at the invitation of C. J. Bartlett, took over Alex Taub's engine responsibilities when he left on a special mission to the United States. He found that most of the troubles that had to be corrected in the months that followed were due to ignorance of the operating conditions that a tank engine had to survive in the field rather than any fundamental faults in the engine itself.

Under the desperate pressure of that post-Dunkirk period, commitments for materials and manufacturing facilities had to be made in advance of prototype testing, in normal circumstances a foolhardy policy but, to quote Platt "When the enemy is at the gate and the defenders lack weapons, engineering prudence is inevitably over-ruled and we had to dive in at the deep end and learn as we went along."

In July 1940, immense further pressure was put on the

C. E. King and Alex Taub with the prototype 12-cylinder tank engine, started for the first time on 11th June 1940, just after Britain had lost most of its existing fleet of tanks with the enforced withdrawal of the British army from Dunkirk. Although most of the troops got out, it was impossible to embark the tanks in time, given the speed of the German advance. So with the country facing a clear threat of invasion, the success of this engine and the tank for which it was intended was vital. It had been designed and built in 89 days.

engineering department, extending far beyond engine matters. The Government decided that Vauxhall was to take over responsibility for the tank itself from Harland & Wolff. This involved taking over the redesign work needed to overcome other known shortcomings of the A20, its testing and the production of the entire tank. This had now been renumbered the A22 following the decision to fit the new engine and the general change of its character.

This was a field of engineering quite different from

An early example of the A22 tank, later known as the Churchill, with temporary wooden cover in place of the turret, takes to the river in Luton Hoo Park, which was used as Vauxhall's testing ground, during the early stages of development. Because of the extreme urgency, production had to begin 'from the drawing board' and before any testing had been done, very much against normal policy for the company or General Motors as a group. Inevitably, a fair amount of trouble was experienced at first, with criticisms being made in Parliament, but even semi-serviceable heavy tanks were better than none. Vauxhall sent an engineer to every Brigade using Churchills, and early tanks in particular were extensively modified to rectify faults, while later output reached much better standards of reliability.

Inevitably, Luton was a target for Luftwaffe bombers, and this reconnaissance photograph was taken on the 25th September 1940, a month after the worst raid on the works, illustrated on the opposite page. It gives detailed information on Luton aerodrome, which may have been considered the main target at that date, when destroying airfields was doubtless still being regarded as a preliminary to invasion, but included the Vauxhall Motors motor works under reference GB 8018, the other number GB 7426 referring to the works of Percival Aircraft Ltd.

anything the Vauxhall team had previously done. The tank's weight alone, of 39 tons in fighting trim, gives an indication that this was a different world – up to 1939, the pressure had been to keep down to an unladen weight of 2 tons 10 cwt for most of Bedford's products. Vauxhall was given a year in which to get the tank into production.

A whole series of shadow factories took on the responsibility for sections of the work, partly to harness enough capacity for the large-scale production envisaged and partly to spread the risk of delay due to any factory being badly damaged by air attack – the most serious raid on Vauxhall was made in August 1940, just as this crucial project was getting under way. So the task of co-ordinating the whole job was yet another problem. The fact that this Herculean task was completed on schedule is a clear indication of the dedication of the many people behind it.

With the prototype engine running reasonably well on the test bed, the attention of the engineering team turned to the tank itself. C. E. King and his assistant, Harold Drew, spent many hours with Government officials trying

to sort out the problems, not helped by the infighting between departments. One of the problems being experienced was in the means of steering – in principle, tanks do so by varying the speed of the left or right tracks and while in theory this could be achieved fairly simply by a system of braking one track or the other, this was not satisfactory on heavy tanks especially if forward speed was to be maintained.

Walter Gordon Wilson, inventor of the preselective epicyclic gearbox, whom C. E. King knew when some prototype gearboxes of this type were fitted to some Vauxhall 14 cars in 1925, had sketched out a mechanism for positive control of steering, by using mechanisms of similar epicyclic type applied to each side of the tank drive, before the war. This idea was taken up by Dr H. E. (Ted) Merritt, who in 1935 had been appointed Chief Engineer of Transmission at the Mechanisation Board, then in charge of tank development, and had started work on applying it in conjunction with the David Brown gear concern in Huddersfield. By then known as the Merritt-Brown

At 4.50pm on Friday, 30th August 1940, just as people would be thinking about getting ready to go home after work, the Vauxhall factory received several direct hits in an air raid. Sadly some 39 people – one woman and 38 men – were killed, and a fair amount of damage to property and vehicles resulted. The top view shows smoke rising immediately after the bombs had fallen, and in the lower views damage to the premises and a military Bedford are shown – note how the blast had distorted the steering wheel and column. Yet by good luck, not one machine tool was seriously affected, and normal production, then running at about 1,000 vehicles per week, was resumed within a few days. Particularly important was the lack of disruption to the work on preparing for production of the Churchill tank and its engine.

transmission, it promised much better control and was to be applied to the A20 and hence inherited by the A22.

A consequence of the appointment of Winston Churchill as Prime Minister was a reorganisation of the Government and this in turn led to many changes in the organisations involved in tank development. The Mechanisation Board vanished and a new Department of Tank Design under the newly formed Ministry of Supply was set up. In May 1940, A. A. M. Durrant, had been seconded from London Transport, where he had been Chief Engineer (Buses and Coaches) and responsible in conjunction with AEC for the design of the RT bus, becoming Director of Research and Development and Controller (Tank Design). Ted Merritt, weary of the infighting, left to join the David Brown concern as Technical Director. Durrant was a more robust character, better suited to dealing with the political infighting – later in the war, he led the team which designed the Centurion tank and after returning to London

**Above left:** Scenes within the factory where bombs had fallen in the 30th August 1940 air raid were fairly chaotic, but concerted effort cleared the collapsed roofing, damaged vehicles and general mess away very quickly so that normal output could resume, if need be even before the buildings were made weatherproof – such events tended, if anything, to make the war effort seem more important.

**Left:** With effort redoubled after the bombing, work on the A22 tank pressed ahead. The decision to name it the Churchill underlined the importance attached to the project, further underlined by this visit in June 1941 by King George VI. He is seen with white coat over the Army uniform he was wearing. The officer wearing a Tank Corps beret was explaining its features. This was one of the first examples to come off the production line, having a 3in howitzer mounted at a low level but with a small 2-pounder gun in the turret, the latter widely criticised for its ineffectiveness and commonly nicknamed 'the peashooter'. Later Marks of the Churchill had much more powerful offensive armament. On the other hand, its armour plate at over 100mm (4in) thick was heavier than most at the time.

On the move, the sheer size of a Churchill was impressive, and even if the speed of 16mph was not all that high, it was enough to kick up the dust in this scene in a Continental village street – the clatter of the tracks would have been deafening, almost drowning the roar of the 350bhp engine. The early problems with the steering had clearly been overcome, allowing the driver confidence in making speed down a street not much wider than the vehicle itself. However, the armament in this case was still of the early type.

Transport was largely responsible for the design of the Routemaster bus.

The Merritt-Brown transmission and steering system was still not right as testing of prototype tanks got under way. On more than one occasion, tanks ran out of control and on one of these some Vauxhall testers had to jump for their lives when a runaway tank took off towards the nearby LMS railway line, fortunately embedding itself in the embankment.

Meanwhile, a new building had been erected in which to build the tanks, the existing premises being fully occupied by production of more conventional Bedford vehicles, then running at almost 1,000 per week. Production of tanks began in July 1941, and a further clue to the importance attached to the project was the decision to give the name Churchill to the A22. That already legendary name would not have been suggested lightly in those days and clearly indicated that it was considered a key element in achieving final victory.

Almost inevitably, the haste with which the Churchill had been conceived was to take its toll in the need to overcome initial unreliability. To quote Maurice Platt's words, "the telescoped Churchill programme produced semi-serviceable heavy tanks very quickly (at a time when the army had none) and fully serviceable tanks came along much more rapidly, and in larger numbers, than anyone had thought possible – to acquit themselves well on many battlefields in 1943 and 1944."

A total of 5,640 tanks were built by Vauxhall and its shadow factories between 1940 and 1945, plus some 2,000 spare engines. The value of giving the job to a firm with expertise in volume production was clear from those figures, and, as Maurice Platt put it "saving factors in the process were the courage and integrity of the King-Drew leadership and the fantastic degree of support and co-operation received from everyone associated with the venture at Vauxhall and elsewhere." Platt was to become Chief Engineer, in succession to C. E. King, in 1953.

Here a later Mark of Churchill, with more powerful gun, is posed with a Vauxhall Ten car, the model from which the Bedford HC 5/6cwt van was derived. The two products from the same factory represented a weight ratio of about 40 to 1.

After proving its worth in Tunisia and Italy, the Churchill was the main British tank involved in the landings in Normandy in 1944. Here some infantrymen hitch a ride on one passing a damaged German tank and a shattered church.

Right: The Churchill was produced in many variants, among the more horrific being the flame thrower, as being demonstrated here.

Foot of page: By contrast, this OWL model, of the type made available to those civilian users who could prove need from 1941, is posed in a peaceful country scene. This was the wartime version of the 5-ton OL as briefly produced in 1939, with civilian wheels and tyres, using twins at the rear, but having the military-style bonnet, complete with crash bar in front of the radiator. This was an OWLD, with dropside body – the addition of a suffix letter to signify the body type was common practice from 1939.

Many of the early production tanks received major modifications very early on in their working lives, but once sorted out, the Churchill established itself as a well-armoured infantry tank. In the desert its speed – 15.5mph on the road – still low by the standards of lighter types, was a disadvantage, but in the Tunisian mountains and Italy it proved invaluable, and in consequence when the Normandy landings were made in 1944, there were more Churchill tanks in use than any other British type. It continued in service until the war ended, and overall fully lived up to its name.

No fewer than 3,000 tanks were re-worked for major design and component changes, some in the process of overcoming the early problems, though many of these were related to updating of armament or conversion for specialised roles. The main series of types ran from Churchill I to Churchill XI, progressing from a 2-pdr gun and 3in howitzer to a 75mm gun, but there were almost innumerable specialised versions, capable of building bridges or laying tracks enabling other vehicles to cross soft ground.

## Other wartime Bedfords

In October 1941, the Government authorised Bedford to produce limited numbers of vehicles for civilian use – goods vehicles and buses of all makes had become virtually unobtainable in the period from 1940, when Britain had stood virtually alone against the strength of the German and Italian armed forces, and the entire nation's production capability had been mobilised to the war effort. The need was still intense, and it was clear that an invasion of Europe would have to be mounted before the war could be won, but the immediate pressure was eased slightly as Germany attacked the Soviet Union in the summer of 1941. Moreover, it was important that makers of war supplies should have reliable transport and also that workers should reach the factories, so there was a need for buses.

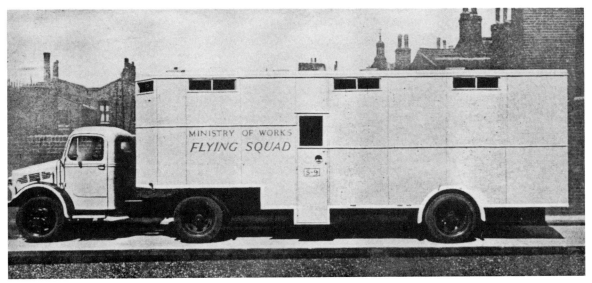

Bedford vehicles had many roles related to the war which were not military. The Ministry of Works Flying Squad artic shown above, using an OXC tractor, was of a type used to convey emergency repair squads to tackle bomb damage repair of an urgent nature. They carried tools and equipment as well as kitchens and sleeping accommodation for the squads. Basically similar bodywork, but with seats and windows, was used in bus form for transport to and within Royal Ordnance factories. The 30-cwt model on military tyres was a mobile canteen used to supply hot meals to bomb victims and rescuers, under a scheme sponsored by the Queen, now the Queen Mother.

Fighting fires, often numerous from the same raid, meant that enormous amounts of hose were used, sometimes of considerable length where water supply was not available near the scene. Getting them back into good order, ready for the next attack, was important, and this hose dryer unit, hauled by an OXC on military-style tyres, was devised for the purpose. During the war, individual fire brigades were merged into the National Fire Service, whose vehicles were painted grey, as seen here.

Three civilian types were produced, under Ministry of Supply control in regard to specification and production, and Ministry of War Transport in regard to allocation, which was only possible on a permit system, giving proof of need. The two goods models were the OWL, which was the long-wheelbase 5-ton model in its wartime guise, with Army-style front and Solex carburettor but 'civilian' wheels – it was available as a dropside truck, OWLD, or with a platform body, OWLE – and the OWS 5-ton tipper, coded OWST with its body. They were built in fair numbers overall, becoming part of the wartime landscape from 1941, though allocations were sparse and few operators received more than a very few at a time.

In addition to these, there were instances of models built to military specification being used in civilian roles, though of a Government-related kind. For example, some OXC 30-cwt models on the 'fat' military tyres were completed as mobile canteens by Spurling and sent to bombed cities to help with immediate food supplies, particularly for rescue workers. The scheme was given personal support by her Majesty the Queen, now the Queen Mother.

Much larger were some articulated buses hauled by OXC tractive units to a design sponsored by the Ministries of Supply and Labour mainly for use within Royal Ordnance Factories, some of which were quite extensive. R. A. Dyson and the British Trailer Co built the trailer underframes and Charles H. Roe built the very utilitarian bodies. The nickname 'Bevin buses' was used for the project, after

Ernest Bevin, the former trade-union leader who was Minister of Labour at the time, but a more ghoulish name was 'coffin bus' due to the shape of the bodywork. Some were 8ft 4in wide, not being subject to normal regulations, carrying 65 passengers on 3+2 seating, though Liverpool Corporation had two dating from 1942, run on public roads serving the Kirkby ROF premises and these were to the normal 7ft 6in width of the time, seating 39 and carrying 26 standing passengers. They were withdrawn and converted to canteens in 1945, possibly acting as the inspiration for the post-war London Transport articulated Bedford-hauled canteens.

The OWB, the standard wartime Bedford bus, of which supplies began to reach operators in 1942, was in a rather different category from other wartime Bedfords, for it was much more closely based on the OB as briefly produced in 1939. It did not have the Army-style front-end, and indeed the appearance of the chassis was very little different from the pre-war model, there being small military-style headlamps, as fitted to many wartime vehicles, and no chromium trim on the radiator grille, which was of the stylish 'bull-nose' type. There were also no chromium bumpers, as common on peacetime Bedford coach models, and although there were pressed covers over the front wheel nuts, these too were painted. Mechanically, the design conformed to the OB specification, and it is significant that even in those days of gloomy austerity, some regard seems to have been paid to the appearance, at least for this passenger model.

The OWB was the only type of new single-deck bus available to British operators under the Ministry of War Transport allocation scheme from 1942 to 1945. This Vauxhall photograph, thought never to have been published previously, shows what was evidently a prototype, probably built in 1941 and virtually certain to have been bodied by Duple. It was generally like the production vehicle but with the emergency door on the offside instead of at the rear and having the benefit of upholstered seats, even if the latter were rather austere-looking. This arrangement allowed for a row of five seats at the rear, so it is possible to account for 29 rearwards of the entrance (and the emergency door directly opposite to it). There would have been room for a pair to the nearside of the driver, as on the production model, but it seems uncertain whether another pair could have been fitted in on the offside immediately behind the driver without infringing the regulations on access to the emergency exit. This latter point may have been why production buses had the emergency exit at the rear, allowing seats for a total of 32 passengers, though by then it had been decided that these would have to be of the wooden slatted type. The finish appears to be the semi-gloss brown primer which was standard on, and peculiar to, the OWB.

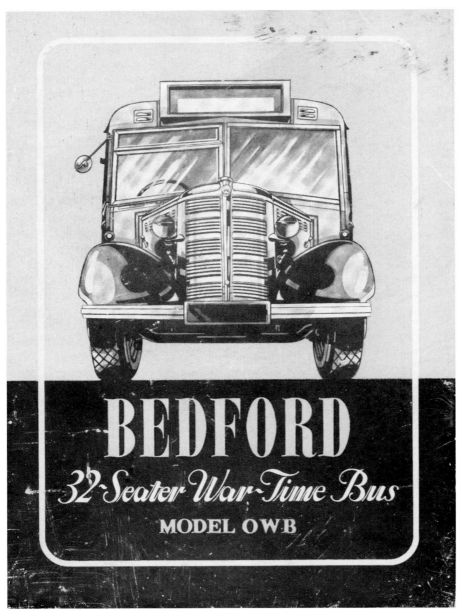

Rather surprisingly, a small sales leaflet was issued for the OWB. This is the front cover, faithful in its rendering of the frontal appearance of the actual vehicle, even if a little glamorous in the way in which it is presented. The appearance of the model designation OWB marked a break with previous policy, possibly caused by its use by the Ministries controlling manufacture and allocation to operators. The wording within was quite frank;-

'This 'economy-type' bus has been built to comply with the wartime specification issued by the Ministry of Supply. The design and fittings are standardized. There are no 'frills' or individual body styles, but the coachwork is durable, workmanlike and serviceable, and all 32 seats are arranged to face forward. Reliability, performance and long life are assured by the Bedford (special) 174in-wheelbase coach chassis.'

This was largely fair comment, the chassis being not unfairly described as a coach chassis, since that was what most of the OB models, which it resembled very closely, were to be. The body quality, like that of most other wartime buses, was let down by the poor quality of wood available. The price, originally quoted at £825 for the complete bus in the semi-gloss brown primer, had been overprinted to read 'Price revised 1.12.42 £800', but had then been revised again by a stick-on label stating that the bus was now fitted with 7.50x20 front tyres and 8.25x20 twin rears, instead of 7.50x20 all round, the price becoming £810. These figures were roughly comparable to those for the glamorous pre-war WTB Vista coach, and in that sort of comparison, so utilitarian a vehicle seemed poor value; indeed it would been virtually unsaleable in 1939, but wartime price inflation was beginning to bite even in 1942. Considered purely as a means of getting 32 people from A to B, it was still very good value by comparison with a typical pre-war heavy-duty bus.

The OWB was supplied with one standard design of body conforming with the 'utility' specification which had then just come into force. It was designed by Duple and provided seats for 32 passengers, albeit tightly spaced and of wooden-slatted construction. The appearance was angular as a result of the requirements of the specification, but at the front, the Duple designers had managed to incorporate windscreens angled in a vee formation with clear affinity to the 1939 goods cab. At the rear, there was a 'shell-back' rear dome and, overall, the finish in general was very austere. The entrance, with folding door, was not directly opposite the driver, and there was one pair of seats ahead of the doorway, always very popular with small boys of whatever age – even if foot-room was somewhat lacking. The majority of the 3,398 built up to late 1945 had bodies built by Duple, though others, tending to be allocated on a

regional basis, were built by Roe, of Leeds, and SMT, in Edinburgh. Later in the war, Mulliner's took over from Roe. All of these were to almost identical design (though the sharp-eyed could detect minute differences), unlike other wartime bus bodies, where each bodybuilding firm used its own interpretation of the utility specifications. They were supplied in a semi-gloss dark brown finish, again uniform from all the bodybuilders involved, in contrast to the utility double-deckers, generally supplied in varying shades of grey.

Most entered service in brown, but depending upon circumstances, some operators painted them in their own livery soon after arrival and a few, unhappy with the wooden seats, fitted replacements from other vehicles. However, one such operator, J. Foster & Son, of Otterburn, deep in rural Northumberland, who put upholstered seats

The standard OWB had tightly-spaced wooden seats providing minimal comfort for 32 passengers, the emergency door being at the rear unlike the prototype on the previous page. This was the 1,000th example about to leave Duple's works in Hendon for delivery. The operator was Bond Bros, of Willington in County Durham, though the Newcastle registration number JTN 915, was doubtless obtained by Adams & Gibbon, the Bedford dealers in that city, through whom it was supplied – even in wartime Bedford operated though its normal dealer organisation for sales to civilian operators. The standard brown finish applied to OWB buses had a gloomy look, although this example appears to have been given a coat of varnish to slightly improve matters – the overall appearance of the type was not unattractive, given the utility specification ban on domed panels. The petrol pump attendant, Mr Jack Watts, was no doubt careful about doling out precious rationed fuel, in those days described as Pool petrol.

The more 'house-proud' operators repainted their OWB buses into standard livery and this could give quite a smart effect. Carruther's of New Abbey ran SW 6596 into Dumfries on a local stage-carriage bus service and it is seen in May 1953 looking very respectable, parked at The Strand in the latter town. The lack of chromium-plated trim was cleverly overcome by picking out parts of the grille in cream.

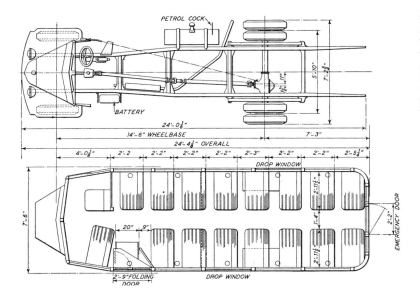

for 28 passengers out of an old bus into one of his OWB buses used on the 32-mile service to Newcastle upon Tyne, promptly got told off by the Regional Traffic Commissioner for reducing the seating capacity – an illuminating example of the bureaucracy which was the downside of wartime life. In fact, the OWB in standard form was not as uncomfortable as might have been thought, at least for someone of medium height, as the hard seats were not too badly shaped in terms of support, and the vehicle suspension, in typical Bedford passenger-model style, was softer-riding than that of most full-sized buses. The smooth engine, with almost silent tickover, was another asset from the passengers' viewpoint, even if the gearbox sound was apt to be obtrusive, especially if well laden.

It had been decided that the Bedford OWB would be the only type of new single-deck bus available to British operators, many of whom used to traditional heavy-duty models as built by such manufacturers such as Leyland, AEC, Daimler or Bristol, viewed the OWB with misgivings, not least because of its light weight, typically 3 tons 6 cwt, and its petrol engine. It was significant that among the larger users were operators with experience of pre-war Bedford models, such as SMT and others of that group, Western and Southern National and Lincolnshire, whose experience of light buses went back to Chevrolet days, though the Leyland Cub had been favoured in the later 1930s.

Many were also supplied to independent operators, most of whom already ran Bedfords and, apart from using them on bus routes, often to country areas, some of these concerns had secured large contracts to carry workers to various factories involved in the war effort. Many of these, quite deliberately, had been located in rural areas to minimise the risk of air raid damage, and were thus not easily reached by existing road or rail services. Some of these operators greatly enlarged their fleets on the basis of the OWB.

Some of the vehicles on rural service were apt to be heavily laden as timetables were restricted to save fuel, and overloading was common then and in the early post-war years, even though officially frowned upon. Alan Townsin recalls one particular journey in an OWB run by M. Charlton & Sons, of Fourstones, near Hexham, over quite a hilly route when the number of passengers being carried on the last journey of the day was 60, nearly half of them standing, and although there were times when the mudguards touched the tyres on bends, there was never any doubt that the game 3.5-litre engine would cope with this load which would have more than filled a contemporary double-decker, even if the gearbox did have to be used more freely than usual.

Many lessons were learned from the harsh treatment many Bedford vehicles, both civilian and military, received in wartime. Some of the earlier examples sent to the Middle East suffered disastrously rapid engine wear in the desert campaigns due to poor filtration of the sand-laden air, overcome fairly quickly by improving the air cleaner efficiency. Exhaust valves were also being burned out at a fairly disastrous rate, but that proved to be at least in part a fuel quality problem related to standardisation on 80 octane fuel with tetra-ethyl lead additive because of American military needs, of which British manufacturers had not been informed, and a change in valve material overcame the difficulty.

All the foregoing, impressive as it is, still does not cover the whole of the Vauxhall/Bedford contribution to the war effort. The demand for spare parts for military vehicles was far greater than would have applied in peacetime, due to the inevitable damage caused by enemy action and the punishing use they received, often driven very hard over poor roads in heat and dust conditions never experienced in normal conditions. Help was sought from the Ministry of Supply in the task of packing and preserving parts required by the Armed Forces.

The following figures of major assemblies give some idea of the vast numbers required and also reflect a tendency to simply replace badly worn or damaged units rather than repair them when facilities and skilled men capable of doing the latter were either not available or engaged on higher-priority work

| WARTIME OUTPUT OF MAJOR ASSEMBLIES | | | |
|---|---|---|---|
| Engines | 228,430 | Front axles | 10,512 |
| Rear axles | 11,149 | Gearboxes | 11,728 |
| Transfer boxes | 3,013 | Steering boxes | 11,459 |

In total, Bedford supplied parts to the value of £18,450,156 between 1939 and 1945. Components were packed in special cases designed to withstand great abuse at a factory in Walsall, Staffordshire, with labour provided by the Ministry of Supply.

Some interesting wartime vehicle designs never went into production, as shown in the separate section, and much important work had even less relation to the company's normal products than the foregoing. Probably the most secret at the time was the work, reckoned to amount to 92%, done on the first twelve jet aircraft engines made in Britain.

On a more mundane level, the company pressed the side panels for five million jerrycans (the pressed-steel fuel containers which got their name from being based on a German design – in wartime, there were no niceties about patents, and it had the advantage of being stackable as well as sturdy). Then there were four million rocket venturi tubes and at one stage the factory was also turning out 6-pounder armour-piercing shells (of a kind which could be used in the guns fitted to some Churchill tanks) at the rate of 5,000 per week. At another, the works rushed out 750,000 steel helmets. A mounting for a 20mm gun was designed and made in seven weeks, going on to make the first 100 by hand methods while tooling up other firms for volume production. There were 4,673 special jigs and dies made for various aircraft and naval construction projects.

Amid all this plethora of work, even the factory itself found it difficult to keep track of all that had been achieved. In a victory parade at the end of the war, a QL carried a placard extolling the output of 209,096 Bedfords supplied to the forces but in fact subsequent checking arrived at a total of 250,000 vehicles supplied for the war effort. The factory employed 12,000 workers and the annual turnover during that period was £22 million.

The Bedford reputation, already high in 1939 after eight short years, was greatly enhanced and became far more widespread as a result of the war. As peace returned after the victories in Europe and then against Japan in 1945, it was time to reap the results from the investment in the new model range made in 1939.

There was some disagreement as to the correct figure for the total of vehicles built during the war. No doubt some of this may come down to the question of just how such vehicles were defined; for example, were the Churchill tanks to be counted as 'Bedfords'? This QL was claimed to be "The 218,249th military Bedford built by Vauxhall", which may not have been quite the same thing as 'Bedfords supplied to the Forces', although it would be understandable if there had been some genuine confusion. In any case the overall total of vehicles built for the war effort, including those supplied for essential civilian use, both goods and passenger, and to various bodies such as the various Ministries, the National Fire Service etc is known to have been roundly 250,000. Regardless of that, there were many such group photographs as this, recording the teams of workers from the various departments who had worked together for long hours, often including week-ends and with very few holidays, and on various shifts, building up strong bonds of loyalty.

## Bedfords that did not make it

As with any large company that produces cars and commercial vehicles, Bedford built a number of prototypes during the war years that never saw production. The 'Giraffe' was an early attempt at getting supplies ashore by way of the beaches before the science of waterproofing engine and ignition systems was fully developed.

The 'Giraffe' was based on the QL with the cab and the engine raised up to a position where the susceptible parts of the engine, including carburettor and distributor, were over seven feet from the ground. The driver of the 'Giraffe' would have enjoyed a spectacular view, being seated ten feet from the ground ! This interesting and original vehicle was capable of driving through water 6ft deep without damage to either vehicle or driver.

Another variation on the QL theme was the Bedford-Bren.

In 1941, with the capture of Singapore by the Japanese, 90% of the world's source of natural rubber was denied to the Allies. In America tremendous efforts were made to develop synthetic rubber as there was a real danger of the stocks of natural rubber running out.

Various attempts were made by manufacturers to reduce the need for natural rubber. With the Bedford Bren this was reduced by 50% by utilising Bren carriers' metal track and suspension in place of the QL's normal rear wheels, axle, and suspension. The vehicle had extremely good cross country performance, superior to many earlier half-track designs.

The Bedford Bren was regarded primarily as a rubber saver. As the supplies of the natural product did not diminish further, it was not considered necessary to put the vehicle into production.

Of all the prototypes produced between 1939 and 1945 technically the most interesting was the BT or Bedford Tractor.

During the 1930s the Germans developed their all-purpose 88mm gun. The gun was extremely mobile due to the type of gun tractor used by the Germans. Throughout the 1930s the German military had tested various designs in order to ascertain the most suitable for the purpose they had in mind. Technically the German three-quarter track gun tractor was very advanced for its time, being steered for example not only by the front wheels but also by the tracks. Both the steering action of the tracks and the front wheels were automatically controlled by a normal steering wheel. When driven on hard surfaces the front wheels steered the vehicle in the normal way, when in soft mud the tracks provided the steering. Eventually the Army captured several of these very useful vehicles and Vauxhalls engineering department was asked to strip the vehicles down, with a view to developing a similar vehicle for the British Army.

Thirteen months later the company had six prototypes running. Various improvements were introduced into the design, with the help of information concerning design faults received from the Intelligence Services on the German originals.

Power was provided by two standard Bedford six-cylinder truck engines which were geared together and developed a combined 140bhp. The Bedford tractor was capable of climbing a hill of 1 in 2 and keeping up an average speed of 25mph fully laden and towing a gun.

By that time the company had gained considerable experience with waterproofing and consequently each Bedford tractor was waterproofed as it was built. In fact the tractor could be driven through 6ft of water without any adverse effect on the engine or chassis.

It was expected that large scale production would commence shortly after the very successful testing of the prototypes.

However, with the successful defeat of the Axis powers in Europe, the project was cancelled, but once again the Luton team had successfully designed the vehicle that was required at the time in only thirteen months.

During the war years the reputation of the company was further enhanced by the performance of Bedford vehicles.

'The Giraffe'. This was an early attempt at a modified QL that could come ashore from a landing craft on to a beach, even if quite deep water was encountered. By lifting up the whole engine, radiator, fuel tank and cab assembly, the problem of a 'drowned-out' engine was eliminated. The type of drive is not recorded but evidently there was a gear, or possibly enclosed chain drive from which a propeller shaft would lead to the transfer box. It would have made a tempting target and the stability over uneven ground and handling with such a high centre of gravity would not have been good.

Below: A half-track QL, known rather confusingly as the Bedford-Bren, really short for Bedford-Bren-carrier, the Bren itself being a light machine-gun, for which the Bren-carrier was a lightweight tracked vehicle. Although apparently planned as a means of reducing demands on rubber, this had good cross-country performance.

At the end of the war, efforts were being made to produce a British equivalent to the very successful type of gun tractor used in large numbers by the German Army. This could logically be described as three-quarter-tracked, though widely called half-track. The Bedford BT is seen on trial in the early months of peace with the Royal Electrical and Mechanical Engineers in the Hartz Mountains, West Germany on April 1946.

The resemblance of the Bedford Tractor or BT to German vehicles of similar type is obvious, particularly in relation to the tracks. No doubt many of the parts were direct copies of what had proved reliable on the German version. However, the style of bonnet has distinct echoes of the Jeep, albeit enlarged to a much greater size. The use of two of the '28hp' Bedford engines, geared together, clearly maintained standardization with the huge numbers of Army Bedford vehicles already in service, even though a single engine giving a similar 140bhp out put would have been more logical for the vehicle considered independently. The sound effects must have been quite interesting.

A whole series of group portrait pictures of the workers in the various departments was taken at the end of the war, in itself a clear indication of what seems to have been 'a happy factory'. This was the one done for the Heavy Vehicle Material Stores, part of the separate establishment set up in 1941 to build the Churchill tanks. Someone with sign-writing ability had gone to the trouble of producing a neatly-written sign. The numbers involved in receiving and issuing the parts to build the tanks gives a clear indication of the scale of the whole enterprise.

# 8 THE POST-WAR BOOM

When the war ended, military contracts ceased almost instantly, but the demand for new vehicles for Bedford's normal customers, and many additional ones, both in Britain and abroad, was immense. With a range that had been extensively updated in 1939, it was largely a matter of picking up where production of those types had left off.

In that sense, Bedford was in a very strong position, with models which still looked very up-to-date and were even better proven after all the wartime experience, so hardly any redesign was to be needed over the major part of the range for five years. Sales demand simply took off, and it was more a matter of producing as many vehicles of the various types as the factory capacity and material supplies would allow. At that time, the tight wartime controls on the whole of industry were still in force, even though now intended to give priority to the most urgent needs in the immediate post-war world, and material shortages were to remain a problem for several years, both of these factors tending to limit output for a time.

In the situation as it stood in 1945, Bedford was also fortunate in the way the most numerous of the company's wartime products were derived from the peacetime Bedford range, so items such as the major parts of engines, gearboxes and axles, as well as frame pressings and many minor parts could be switched to the civilian range with no more than minor change, even though the visual differences of the return to the bull-nose radiator and tapered bonnet, civilian tyre sizes etc made the peacetime product look very different.

Hence, Bedford models to peacetime specification began production almost immediately after military production ended, during the latter part of 1945, in most cases having the same specifications and model designations as introduced in mid-1939.

There was a change in the method of distinguishing the 5-ton models from the 3-4-ton models on which they were based. Instead of the addition of '/40' to the designation for the 5-ton versions (so that, as an example, a 1939 5-tonner with dropside body was designated OLD/40), the letter 'A' for 3-4-ton or 'B' for 5-ton was added just after the 'length' letter, the 5-ton dropside becoming OLBD, while a similar 3-ton model would be OLAD. The short chassis similarly became OSA or OSB, with appropriate body letter added, such as OSBT for a 5-ton tipper. Another clarification in terms of type was the use of OSS for the Bedford-Scammell tractive unit version, complete with cab.

Bedford models of this period, from the 30-40-cwt up to 5-ton categories, were built as bare chassis, which took the suffix letter Z; chassis with cab, suffix C; dropside truck, suffix D; complete dropside truck, suffix D; complete end-tipper truck, suffix T.

The 5-ton models became very popular, just as the earlier maximum-load versions of Bedford models had done, since the extra capability cost very little more either in first cost or running costs compared to the 3-4-ton

There was a strong emphasis on exports in the post-war world. Uganda Transport Co Ltd, part of the large Overseas Motor Transport Co Ltd group operating in various parts of Africa, took delivery of 30 buses with special Duple bodies at the beginning of 1946 – they had upholstered seats for eight in the first-class compartment at the front and 20 in the 2nd class at the rear on slatted seats, very like the type used on wartime buses in Britain. The central bar on the roof was provided for the carriage of bicycles. The small headlamps and lack of chromium trim indicate that this one awaiting delivery from Duple was on an OWB chassis, though it differed from home market examples in having a second petrol tank, bringing the total capacity to 40 gallons.

versions. Vehicle operators of all types were themselves busy as the country set about catching up with work postponed due to the war, created by the aftermath of the war itself and, in particular, responding to the Government's exhortation to export more of the nation's products. Bedford played its full part in this latter, the 10,000th post-war export example going to Istanbul as early as October 1946, barely a year after civilian production was resumed. Left-hand-drive versions of virtually all models were produced in quite large numbers and wartime operation gave Bedford valuable experience in ensuring that vehicles were offered in specifications appropriate to overseas conditions, though the general principle was to so design models that they would cope with most circumstances in standard form.

There had been softening, literally, of the full rigours of the wartime specification of the standard OWB wartime 32-seat bus, in which upholstered seats had begun to be fitted from early 1945. Then, during the winter of 1945-6, the last OWB chassis began to receive what Duple christened its Mark II bus body, of the same capacity and layout as the utility version, but of greatly improved appearance, with only the minor details such as the wartime-pattern headlamps to give the clue to the fact that the chassis were still to wartime specification.

This same body continued on the OB chassis when production of that resumed, and thus the distinction between

**Exports of Bedford vehicles had been quite numerous before the war, but in the post-war world, with strong Government pressure because of the need to improve Britain's financial position in the world, they became much larger, despite the urgent need for new vehicles in Britain. Here an OLB model is well laden with sacks of wool in New Zealand.**

In succession to the wartime OWB with its utility body, Duple introduced a design of bus following the same layout but with greatly improved appearance, given the name 'Mark II'. Some were built on late OWB chassis but this one was on the OB, and although evidently in the characteristic dark brown, appears to have been built to an export specification, with 'louvred louvres', in other words small ventilating slots pressed into the rain strips over the windows. The windscreen, divided into main and upper panels on both sides, was also non-standard. The window sticker gives the bodybuilder's name as Duple Bodies & Motors Ltd, which dates this photograph as during the earlier part of 1946, the title changing that year to Duple Motor Bodies Ltd.

Examples of the OB with Duple Mark II bus body became quite a familiar sight in the first year or so after the war, Lincolnshire Road Car Co Ltd in effect continuing its wartime use of the OWB with examples of the post-war equivalent. The home-market model had an opening driver's windscreen, needed at that date to conform to PSV regulations, but as with the OWB, the deeper nearside panel was fixed.

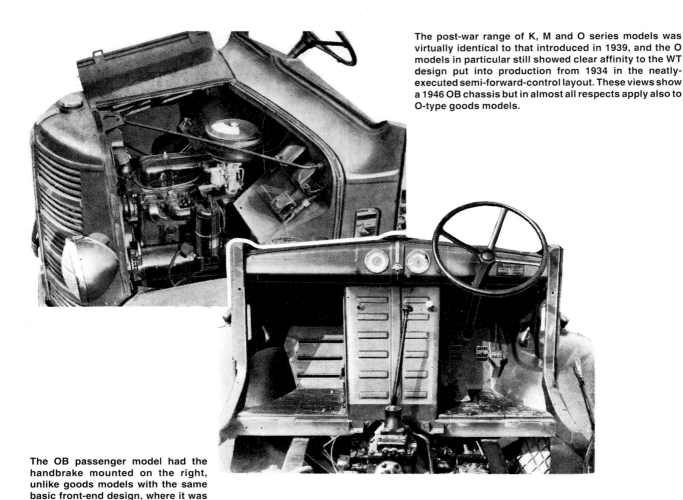

The post-war range of K, M and O series models was virtually identical to that introduced in 1939, and the O models in particular still showed clear affinity to the WT design put into production from 1934 in the neatly-executed semi-forward-control layout. These views show a 1946 OB chassis but in almost all respects apply also to O-type goods models.

The OB passenger model had the handbrake mounted on the right, unlike goods models with the same basic front-end design, where it was positioned in the centre.

the two chassis versions was shown to amount to quite trivial details. In later years, many OWB chassis were rebodied and, in the process, received post-war headlamps and chromium trim details, becoming indistinguishable from the post-war product. Somewhat confusingly, the utility body design, only slightly modified with a rounded rear dome and no indicator box, was built on the new OB chassis in some numbers for the Royal Air Force in 1946.

Early in 1946, the first OB models with the post-war Duple Vista coach body appeared, and another legendary Bedford success story was taken to new heights. It was the first coach body to appear on the British market after six weary years of war, during which a new coach with curvaceous styling and most of the features associated with a vehicle designed for pleasure travel had become no more than a memory. The only slightly sub-standard feature of the earlier examples was the type of seating, which, though high backed and relatively comfortable, was based on a tubular steel frame of the same nature as widely used for bus seats at the time, and hence did not quite look the part. That was put right a couple of years or so later when a revised design, still steel-framed but altered so that the top of the frame was used as a handrail, appeared.

When its forthcoming availability was first announced, it was indicated that the coach would be a 26-seater, following the practice of the late 1930s, but a change from the pre-war method of taxing passenger vehicles (which had meant that anything over 26-seat capacity would be taxed at the same rate as a 32-seater) led to 27-seat and 29-seat versions being offered. The overall length of coaches of this class tended to vary slightly from type to type, but most OB coaches were a foot or more longer than the WTB model with which most Bedford coach operators had ended in 1938-9, and almost immediately it tended to be the 29-seat model that was the more usual choice, with a minority favouring 27, perhaps for touring duty where more leg-room was thought desirable.

The chassis price of the OB in May 1946 was £440, reflecting wartime inflation, the 32-seat Mark II bus £1,140, and the coach, quoted at that stage as a 26-seater though few if any were actually built thus, at £1,265, the 29-seater costing only £10 more. The value was still very competitive, and once again, even the chassis of a typical heavy-duty model was priced higher than the complete OB Vista coach. The demand outstripped supply, and in a repeat of wartime practice, the SMT concern built Vista bodies to Duple design for a time, these tending to go to Scottish or north of England operators, though the numbers

When the post-war Duple Vista coach body first appeared, it seemed like a breath of fresh air after the years of wartime austerity, when no new coaches were being made. The resumption of coach excursions and tours was another sign of relief from the privations which continued into the post-war period. Here three OB Vista coaches of Greenslades Tours Ltd of Exeter are about to depart on a day tour from Exeter to what was described as the 'English Switzerland' in 1948. The post-war Vista had some resemblances to the final pre-war designs of 1939-40, but the front end of the body was different, and with the set-back entrance door, there was space for a pair of forward-facing seats at the nearside front, always popular with passengers.

On the offside of the Vista, a relatively small emergency door was set further forward than the entrance door was on the nearside. It had a signalling window for the driver and in effect it could almost be regarded as a driver's door, though hardly ever used as such. The Vista was found in fleets of almost all types, this one dating from early 1948 belonging to Lincolnshire and still looking very smart when seen in Skegness in July 1954.

Notable among bus bodywork on the OB chassis was the lightweight design produced by J. C. Beadle of Dartford for several of the Tilling group operating companies. This is a 1949 example in the fleet of Hants & Dorset Motor Services Ltd, seen under municipal trolleybus overhead wires near The Square, Bournemouth. Parked on the right is a Bournemouth Corporation Bedford WTB, one of the 1938 batch of twelve which had Burlingham 25-seat bodies built to a design very like the Duple Hendonian body of that period.

of these were not very large and Duple versions were being delivered country-wide.

Many other bodybuilders produced bodies on the OB, in a variety of styles; some built in fair numbers, but the Vista was by far the most popular. The Mark II bus soon became no more than a minority choice, just as had been the case pre-war, and for a time this design was produced by Mulliners Ltd, an association with the building of bus bodywork for Bedford chassis that was to continue for many years, notably for military contracts.

For many years, right up to the 1960s, it was normal to glance in the yard of almost any village coach operator and

The demand for coach bodywork in the immediate post-war period was such that many small bodybuilders entered the market, some producing very professional designs. Pearson of Liverpool was one of these, and this body style was built in modest numbers on the Bedford OB chassis for various operators. This one had been new to Fallowfield & Britten of London in 1947, but is seen some years later when operating for Tillingbourne Valley. The design is a little reminiscent of the pre-war Duple Vista in regard to its relatively broad windscreen.

Plaxton was still one of the smaller bodybuilding concerns in the early post-war years, but built quite a number of coach bodies on OB chassis. Some were on the standard chassis but others were converted to forward-control in a manner found occasionally on pre-war Plaxton coaches on Bedford chassis. The driving position was moved forward and the windscreen positioned just behind the radiator grille, requiring a larger cowl within the vehicle, though the gear lever was not altered, requiring the driver to reach back somewhat when changing gear. This example seated 30, which was the usual maximum, and the amount of modification to gain just one extra passenger seat compared to the usual 29 seems a disproportionate effort. This example was for A. Martlew & Sons, of Donnington Wood. Shropshire, dating from June 1947. The interior, in what might nowadays be described as Art Deco style, was rather let down by the grab handles crudely attached to the seats by wood screws.

This 30/40-cwt van was a catalogued model, the body being built by Spurling. It fitted neatly into the range, its styling being very much in keeping with that of the goods vehicles, not only having the vee windscreen (the chassis being supplied in 'chassis scuttle' form and with the cab doors), but also having a waistline moulding of the same form. The standard van had two hinged doors at the rear, but an alternative version had sliding doors on each side giving access to the load-space, claimed to amount to 232 cu ft. It was built on a hardwood frame, using steel panels.

At the other end of the scale was this furniture van, based on an OB passenger chassis, for Maple & Co Ltd, the leading furniture store having shops in Tottenham Court Road, London; Birmingham; Bournemouth; Brighton; Nottingham and Leeds. This body was also built by Spurling, and although constrained to use a relatively upright profile, the windscreen layout was still of vee-form. The OB's chromium-plated bumpers and hub caps suited the image of a high-class concern – it is noteworthy that it was still displaying the royal coat of arms and 'By appointment to the late King George V' lettering although he had died in 1935.

The Bedford-Lacre sweeper-collector used a left-hand drive 2/3ton chassis so as to allow the driver to sweep right up to the kerb — he was given an extra mirror, attached to the main rear view mirror but set at an angle giving a direct view downwards. Water jets under the front bumper allowed the road to be dampened, and the sweeping brush was followed by another to lift leaves or other road dirt into the rear part of the body. Lacre used to make its own small three-wheeled sweeper using the same basic principles but it was more economic when scaling it up to use proprietary chassis.

see an OB Vista, and they were also to be found in many larger fleets, including quite a few where Bedford models had never been seen before.

Variety of bodywork was also evident on goods models, even though the factory-built dropside and tipper versions were the most widely seen. Spurling produced an attractive van on the 30/40-cwt K-type, using the windscreen and doors from the standard cab, and this was listed in Bedford literature as a standard model — it offered a useful load space of 232 cubic feet.

On the whole range, other bodybuilders offered vans of widely varying types right up to roomy pantechnicons (these latter sometimes built on the OB passenger chassis), cattle-trucks, horse-boxes, ambulances, tankers, refuse collectors, gulley emptiers....the list is almost endless. Users varied from owner-drivers with one vehicle to huge

fleets run by household names or big haulage firms.

The smaller car-related van range restarted production in 1946, when the HC 5/6-cwt and the JC 10/12-cwt models reappeared, alongside the Vauxhall Ten, Twelve and Fourteen cars with which they shared much of their structure and major units, including the independent front suspension. It had been decided to rationalise production of the two four-cylinder cars, the Ten and Twelve, using a common body shell, derived from the 1940 Ten model, which had been slightly larger than the original 1937 design. This meant that effectively, the difference between the two was simply the choice of engine, and it was decided to give the HC van the 1,442cc Twelve engine.

An alteration of Government policy, abandoning the 'horse power' tax on cars related to the RAC rating, partly to encourage the production of models with larger engines

Special-purpose bodywork gradually evolved to meet specific needs. For example, this 2/3-ton ML of 1950 had bodywork designed to cope with moving crates of bottles for Seven-Up Bottling Co Ltd of Chiswick. With the body divided vertically and each side inclined inwards loads were sufficiently secure for local transport, and the section ahead of the rear axle was at a lower level. Transatlantic influence both in choice of beverages and eye-catching liveries was more evident after the war, but Bedford vehicles of this period looked well in most styles.

which it was thought would sell better abroad, led to the dropping of the Ten and its 1,203cc engine completely in 1947.

The next step on the car side was the introduction of two new models in October 1948. These were the Wyvern, type LIX, again having the 1,442cc engine, and the Velox, type LIP, with a new six-cylinder 2,275cc, though both had essentially the same body shell, essentially a revamped version of the previous four-cylinder shell derived from the 1940 Ten, though with new front-end with headlamps moved to the front wings and a wider low-level horizontal-bar grille. Three-speed gearboxes were standard, as had been so in all new Vauxhall car designs since 1937, but a new feature was the then fashionable steering-column gear-change.

At this point the HC van was dropped, and the 10/12-cwt moved on from the JC to the PC, retaining the 105in (8ft 9in) wheelbase and much of the previous model's general design, including the appearance as first introduced in 1939. It is noteworthy that although the structure of the front-end was all-metal up to and including the side doors, the rear of the body was based on a hardwood frame with sheet-steel panelling. With this model Bedford reverted to its pre-war practice of allowing van styling to lag behind that for cars – by 1952, when the model was superseded,

it was beginning to look a little dated, though not as much as the previous BYC had done in 1939.

The PC retained the 1,442cc engine, but adopted the steering-column gearchange, as on the L-series cars. This latter feature was one of many ideas picked up by the British car industry – not only Vauxhall – from an American trend which was understandable in the days of bench front seats, but had little merit on a smaller car and even less on a van. Another new feature, reversing previous Vauxhall/Bedford trends, was a 12-volt electrical system – larger Bedford models, save for the OB, were still using 6-volt systems. As usual at that time, emphasis was put on fuel economy, a test by *The Commercial Motor* being quoted as returning 39mpg with an 11cwt load at an average speed of 28.8mph. Useful load space was quoted as 110 cubic feet, the unladen weight being 18 cwt in taxation condition and the maximum gross laden weight 1 ton 12 cwt 1 qr.

The 10/12-cwt model had been available since wartime with a passenger conversion, the Utilecon, made by Martin, Walter Ltd, a bodybuilding firm based at Folkestone which had specialised in building cabriolet bodies on Vauxhall cars in the 1930s. It introduced the Utilecon as an alternative line of business and picked up an idea that had been tried on the original VYC version of the 10/12-cwt van in the early 1930s, with quickly-stowable seats for seven

The makers of 'Merry Monk' canned goods, I. Beer & Sons Ltd, with headquarters in London, chose a van body for this 2/3-ton ML, also dating from 1950, lettered in a more traditional style.

This 1946 OLB 5-ton lorry, operated by the world-famous concern of Josiah Wedgwood & Sons of Stoke-on-Trent, had seen a few years service when chosen for this publicity stunt, poised delicately on four of that firm's china tea cups, with London's Tower Bridge as a backdrop. Whilst looking impressive from that point of view, it was perhaps also a reminder of how the weight of this model was kept down so as to allow operation at 30mph when heavier models were still restricted to 20mph. The fitting of fog lamps on both this vehicle and the van shown above is a reminder that fog, or smoke-based 'smog' was still a regular hazard in those days before the Clean Air Act controlled the use of coal in countless open fires, as well as the emission of industrial smoke. It is a pity someone forgot to adjust the driver's mirror.

By 1950, the first-generation Bedford models had largely disappeared from the major fleets, but were still to be found in smaller undertakings in the more remote areas. This scene in the Newtown workshops of Mid-Wales Motorways shows UN 7783, a 1934 WLB, evidently in for minor attention but still having that indefinable look of being a well-cared-for vehicle, incidentally having a pair of front tyres with plenty of tread on them, by no means always so even on big operators' buses in those days. On the right, a WTB with what looks like a Duple K. D. body of c1936 receives attention to the emergency door, which may well have dropped somewhat over the years, while a seat is repaired in the foreground. Clearly, these were old-style craftsmen, and at that stage even rural bus operation could pay its way even if no money-spinner, such was the demand for bus travel.

passengers which allowed the van to be used as a load-carrier 'in 30 seconds', it was claimed. The Royal Navy had a number of these in service in wartime, but the postwar version was sold more widely, as a school bus, means of carrying workers to and from sites etc. The firm later moved on to other convertible types of vehicle, very often Bedford-based, and eventually was renamed Dormobile, after possibly its most famous product, which we shall meet in the second volume.

A noteworthy milestone was reached on 22nd October, 1947, when the half-millionth Bedford produced at Luton was driven off the assembly line by the Minister of Supply. Also in the cab was the Bedford employee who had driven off the first Bedford in early 1931. Of that output, almost exactly half had been built in wartime, but at that date, examples of Bedford models of all generations right back to the beginning were still a common sight. The early types with radiator directly over the front axle were looking decidedly old-fashioned by the post-war era, but the WT-series and subsequent models tended to be regarded as only mildly different from current models, as in many respects was so, and remained in use in large numbers up to well into the 1950s.

In normal times, inexpensive commercial vehicles tend not to have long lives, but many had them extended because of the war and even when new models became generally available, it took some time to catch up with demand. In many cases, the new vehicles were wanted for expansion of thriving businesses, and the older ones simply remained in service. Bedford models were relatively straightforward to overhaul and repair and the fact that two basic engine designs covered all models, apart from the small vans, from 1931 to 1950 made doing so a much more simple task than for models of makes built in much smaller quantities.

In addition to the service offered by Bedford dealers covering much of the country, there were specialist firms specialising in the overhaul of Bedford engines and other units. Hamilton Motors (London) Ltd, trading as HML Engineering, with premises in Edgware Road and Harrow Road, offered rebuilt Bedford engines on an exchange basis, operating on a large scale and advertising regularly in the trade press.

In March 1950, a series of improvements were

(continued on page 144

Bedford buses and coaches continued to be in favour with Mid-Wales Motorways. This trio of OB models included two, EP 9548 on the right with Mark II bus body and EP 9588 on the left with Vista coach body, which were new to Mid-Wales in 1946-7. The vehicle in the centre, MHU 49, was new to the Bristol Tramways & Carriage Co Ltd in 1949, withdrawn by its successor, Bristol Omnibus Co Ltd, in 1958 and sold via a dealer to Mid-Wales in February 1959. Note how the appearance of the Duple bus body had altered between 1946 and 1949, with more inward taper towards the front, giving a windscreen outline more akin to that of the Vista. The author's trips to Chesham Preparatory School at Lye Green in the late 1940s were in OBs similar to these but with Thurgood bodies.

Hard-working Bedford models dating from the early post-war years were an everyday sight through the succeeding decade. This OL, almost certainly an OLBD 5-ton model, of the North British Locomotive Co Ltd was registered late in 1949. It was about nine years old when seen in one of its owner's works in Glasgow in the Spring of 1958, having brought a pair of driving wheels for final erection of a shunting locomotive, probably that on the left of the picture. In the background are two of British Railways first batch of Warship class 2,000bhp diesel-hydraulic locomotives for the Western Region.

Despite the association of Greenslades Tours Ltd of Exeter with luxury travel, it was still using several OWB models for some years after the war, though they had been rebuilt to tone down the 'utility' look, fitted with upholstered seats and sliding roofs. Three of them, dating from about 1943, can be seen alongside a pair of OB Vistas in this garage view in May 1948. Two have received larger chromium-plated headlamps while the third has had the originals chromed.

London Transport had ten of these Bedford-Scammell articulated mobile canteens, JXC 9 being the last to enter service, in 1949. After being pensioned off from service in the capital, four of them saw further service with Liverpool Corporation, and the vehicle is seen performing its role in Castle Square. They gave 24 years of service split equally between the two operators.

Despite the large numbers of Bedford passenger models with the familiar Duple Vista body, there was still considerable variety. British Railways placed this 20-seat bus on OLAZ 2/3-ton chassis in service in 1950 to convey train crews on the Western Region. It had OB suspension and the body was by All-Weather Motor Bodies Ltd. It could be regarded as a later-generation equivalent of the early WLB-model buses of similar capacity.

At the other end of the scale was this OB, another example of the Australian fondness for a stretched-wheelbase. Despite the length, this Royal Mail bus seated only twelve passengers, carried in the front compartment, the rear being devoted to carrying mail on a route between Woodenbong and Killarney in Queensland.

Above and below: The Overseas Touring Co (East Africa) Ltd, of Nairobi, was another subsidiary of the United Transport group. This special Duple body on OB chassis was supplied in 1946. The body was clearly designed to have the appearance of a private car of the period, with body tapering inwards at the front so as to almost merge with the line set by the bonnet side panels and having a single-panel windscreen and swept mudguards. Within there were luxurious Christie-Tyler seats of a type then newly developed for aircraft use, set in a two-and one arrangement.

Above: From the three-quarter rear view, there was more than a slight hint of Vauxhall car designs of the mid-1930s. The drop-down boot lid gave access to a luggage area within the interior of the vehicle – there were no seats aft of the rear axle. Twin fuel tanks were provided, as on other United Transport Bedford vehicles for service in Africa.

A slightly less ambitious 14-seat body design, closer to the standard Vista, was produced for Overseas Touring Co (East Africa) Ltd in 1947, though even this had wider pillar spacing rearwards of the entrance door, and a more swept tail. In this case, the seats were of a more orthodox design, but all had armrests and the plain leather facings looked very inviting.

Meanwhile, standard Duple Vista bodies on OB chassis continued to be produced with very little variation for the home market. A minor change evident on this early 1949 example, one of a batch of eight for Crosville Motor Services Ltd, is the chromium-plated Duple motif on the bonnet side. Some 12,693 OB models had been built when production ceased in November 1950.

(Continued from page 138)

announced to the standard '28hp' engine, given the name Extra Duty. By that date Maurice Platt was in charge of engine design and R. R. Bishop in charge of commercial vehicle design. It was still of the same $3\frac{3}{8}$in bore and 4in stroke, 3.519-litre capacity and 27.34hp RAC rating as when first introduced in 1938. By then, over 400,000 such engines had been produced for use in production Bedford chassis, in itself a measure of the degree to which the slogan 'You see them everywhere' was even more justifiable than when it had been introduced. At that date, apart from the inevitable war casualties among the military types, the great majority of Bedford vehicles with this power unit were still in service.

The Extra Duty version of the engine gave more power; the version fitted to 3-4-ton, 5-ton, Bedford-Scammell and the OB passenger model, fitted with a larger carburettor, now had a power output of 84bhp at 3,100rpm, instead of the 72bhp at 3,000rpm of the earlier version. The 30-cwt and 2-3-ton models, now fitted with a slightly smaller carburettor, went up more slightly, to 76bhp. These power ratings conformed to standard American practice in being taken from units without fan, with ignition adjusted for maximum power and a workshop exhaust system, but the net figures with standard accessories and exhaust, as preferred by *The Commercial Motor*, still showed a useful

increase from 68.5bhp to 80bhp for the full-rated engine. Maximum net torque went up more marginally from 164lb-ft to 166lb-ft, but continued to be at 1,000rpm, showing that the willingness to pull at low speeds which had always been a characteristic, had not been sacrificed.

Probably of more practical benefit to the operator were the features designed to improve engine life. There was a switch to copper-lead main and big-end bearings in place of the previous white metal, and the crankshaft became induction hardened, while improved cylinder bore finish was coupled with the use of chromium-plated top piston rings. There were also improved air and oil filters and a positive ventilation system for the crankcase. *The Commercial Motor* road test on an OLBD 5-ton example gave 13.5mpg running fully laden on simulated long-distance haulage and 11.2mpg on local work with more stops.

Study of a brochure issued when the Extra Duty engined models were announced reveals that by then two maximum gross weights were being quoted for most Bedford models,

**Opposite page:** This summary of the model range as offered at the time of the introduction of the Extra Duty engine indicates its extent and how, though usefully improved, in basic terms it was still much as had been introduced in 1939, save that the 5/6-cwt van had been dropped.

The cutaway drawing of the Extra Duty version of the 28hp engine shown below appeared in a brochure on the revised range of models issued in March 1950. Several of the features picked out were already incorporated in production engines, but the revised engines gave a blend of exceptionally well-proven design. Over 400,000 examples of the type built, with improvements to extend engine life as well as a useful increase in power.

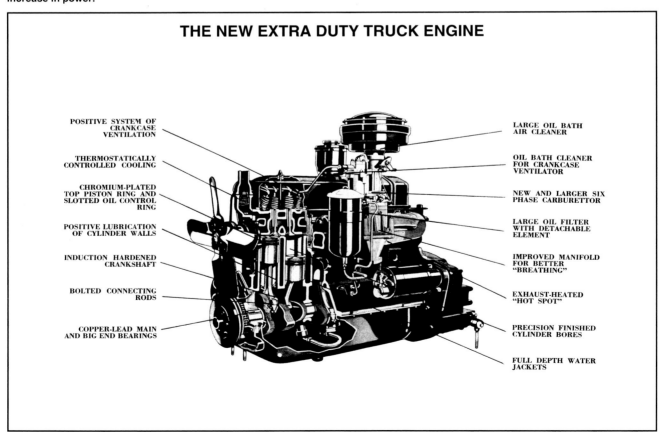

## THE NEW EXTRA DUTY TRUCK ENGINE

POSITIVE SYSTEM OF CRANKCASE VENTILATION

THERMOSTATICALLY CONTROLLED COOLING

CHROMIUM-PLATED TOP PISTON RING AND SLOTTED OIL CONTROL RING

POSITIVE LUBRICATION OF CYLINDER WALLS

INDUCTION HARDENED CRANKSHAFT

BOLTED CONNECTING RODS

COPPER-LEAD MAIN AND BIG END BEARINGS

LARGE OIL BATH AIR CLEANER

OIL BATH CLEANER FOR CRANKCASE VENTILATOR

NEW AND LARGER SIX PHASE CARBURETTOR

LARGE OIL FILTER WITH DETACHABLE ELEMENT

IMPROVED MANIFOLD FOR BETTER "BREATHING"

EXHAUST-HEATED "HOT SPOT"

PRECISION FINISHED CYLINDER BORES

FULL DEPTH WATER JACKETS

# A BEDFORD FOR EVERY LOAD AND PURPOSE UP TO 8 TONS

## 10-12 CWT. VAN

Wheelbase, 105 in. (8 ft. 9 in.).
12 h.p., 4 cyl. engine.
Max. Gross Weight, 1 ton 12¼ cwt.
Capacity of Van, 110 cubic feet plus
10 cu. ft. by driver.

## 30 CWT. & AMBULANCE

Wheelbase 120 in. (10 ft. 0 in.).
76 b.h.p., 6 cyl. engine.
Max. Gross Weight, Chassis and
Tyre Rating, 4 tons 0 cwt.

## 2-3 TON SHORT

Wheelbase 120 in. (10 ft. 0 in.).
76 b.h.p., 6 cyl. engine.
*Max. Gross Weight
Chassis Rating, 5 tons 10 cwt.
Tyre Rating, 5 tons 5 cwt.

## 2-3 TON LONG

Wheelbase 143 in. (11 ft. 11 in.)
76 b.h.p., 6 cyl. engine.
*Max. Gross Weight
Chassis Rating, 5 tons 13 cwt.
Tyre Rating, 5 tons 5 cwt.

## 3-4 TON SHORT

Wheelbase 111 in. (9 ft. 3 in.).
84 b.h.p., 6 cyl. engine.
*Max. Gross Weight
Chassis Rating, 7 tons 10 cwt.
Tyre Rating, 6 tons 15 cwt.

## 3-4 TON LONG

Wheelbase 157 in. (13 ft. 1 in.).
84 b.h.p., 6 cyl. engine.
*Max. Gross Weight
Chassis Rating, 7 tons 10 cwt.
Tyre Rating, 6 tons 15 cwt.

## 5 TON SHORT

Wheelbase 111 in. (9 ft. 3 in.).
84 b.h.p., 6 cyl. engine.
*Max Gross Weight
Chassis Rating, 8 tons 14 cwt.
Tyre Rating, 8 tons 5 cwt.

## 5 TON LONG

Wheelbase 157 in. (13 ft. 1 in.).
84 b.h.p., 6 cyl. engine.
*Max. Gross Weight
Chassis Rating, 8 tons 14 cwt.
Tyre Rating, 8 tons 5 cwt.

## PASSENGER CHASSIS

Wheelbase 174 in. (14 ft. 6 in.).
84 b.h.p., 6 cyl. engine.
*Max. Gross Weight
Chassis Rating, 7 tons 3 cwt.
Tyre Rating, 7 tons 0 cwt.

## 8 TON BEDFORD SCAMMELL

Special Bedford tractor for articulated trailers·
84 b.h.p., 6 cyl. engine.
*Max. Gross Train Weight, 12 tons.

145

one being called the chassis rating and another, rather lower, the rating with standard tyres. The 5-ton models had a chassis rating of 8 tons 14 cwt, but this came down to 8 tons 5 cwt as a rating with standard tyres. Similar remarks applied in varying degree to other models, it being clear that tyre ratings were the practical limiting factor, and there was growing awareness of the dangers of overloading of tyres.

The gross weight figures for the 30-cwt model were quoted as 4 tons both as a chassis rating and tyre rating, and this may give an indication as to why that model was no longer described as 30/40cwt, that designation having been dropped in October 1948. Although the 2-ton loading appears to have still been possible within the 4-ton gross limit on a typical dropside model weighing 1 ton 15 cwt 1 qr, the load, carried very largely on the rear axle, may have been too much in practice for the single rear tyres. At the same time, Spurling introduced an optional van version with sliding side doors to give easier access to the load space, these extra doors being behind the standard hinged cab doors.

The table on the opposite page gives details of the Bedford range as it stood in the spring of 1950:-

**The short-wheelbase tipper had always been an important part of the Bedford range, and this illustration of the 4 cubic yard body offered in either 3/4-ton OSAT or 5-ton OSBT form appeared in the March 1950 brochure.**

**The 2/3-ton tipper, type MST, had a shallower body with 2.75 cubic yard capacity, and had hand-operated tipping gear, unlike the hydraulic operation standard on the heavier-duty model.**

## BEDFORD MODELS AND PRICES, SPRING 1950

| Code | Model | Body | Wheelbase | Price |
|------|-------|------|-----------|-------|
| PC | 10/12-cwt | Van | 8ft 9in | £325 |
| PC | 10/12-cwt | Utilecon (7-seat/van) | 8ft 9in | £430 |
| KZ | 30-cwt | Chassis | 10ft 0in | £359 |
| | 30-cwt | Ambulance chassis | 10ft 0in | £379 |
| | 30-cwt | Van (Spurling) | 10ft 0in | £526 |
| KC | 30-cwt | Chassis cab | 10ft 0in | £398 |
| KD | 30-cwt | Dropside truck | 10ft 0in | £431 |
| MSZ | 2-3-ton | Chassis | 10ft 0in | £393 |
| MSC | 2-3-ton | Chassis cab | 10ft 0in | £432 |
| MSD | 2-3-ton | Dropside truck | 10ft 0in | £468 |
| MST | 2-3-ton | End Tipper (hand operated) | 10ft 0in | £488 |
| MLZ | 2-3-ton | Chassis | 11ft 11in | £405 |
| MLC | 2-3-ton | Chassis cab | 11ft 11in | £444 |
| MLD | 2-3-ton | Dropside truck | 11ft 11in | £484 |
| OSAZ | 3-4-ton | Chassis | 9ft 3in | £451 |
| OSAC | 3-4-ton | Chassis cab | 9ft 3in | £490 |
| OSAT | 3-4-ton | End tipper (hydraulic) | 9ft 3in | £590 |
| OLAZ | 3-4-ton | Chassis | 13ft 1in | £461 |
| OLAC | 3-4-ton | Chassis cab | 13ft 1in | £500 |
| OLAD | 3-4-ton | Dropside truck | 13ft 1in | £565 |
| OSBZ | 5-ton | Chassis | 9ft 3in | £482 |
| OSBC | 5-ton | Chassis cab | 9ft 3in | £521 |
| OSBT | 5-ton | End tipper (hydraulic) | 9ft 3in | £621 |
| OLBZ | 5-ton | Chassis | 13ft 1in | £492 |
| OLBC | 5-ton | Chassis cab | 13ft 1in | £531 |
| OLBD | 5-ton | Dropside truck | 13ft 1in | £596 |
| OSS | | Bedford-Scammell chassis cab | 9ft 3in | £490 |
| OB | Bus or coach | Chassis | 14ft 6in | £533 |
| OB | Bus | Duple Mk IV 30-seat | 14ft 6in | £1,571 |
| OB | Coach | Duple Vista 27-seat | 14ft 6in | £1,725 |
| OB | Coach | Duple Vista 29-seat | 14ft 6in | £1,736 |

The output of Vauxhall Motors Ltd, taken as an organisation making both its cars and Bedford commercial vehicles, had risen steadily in the 1930s, from a combined total of 14,836 in 1931 and reaching a production highpoint in 1939, with 61,454 vehicles. This figure reflects lively sales of both cars and commercials up to that last peacetime summer, doubtless invigorated by new models almost across the board, and then military contracts coming in strongly in the latter part of the year. The 1940 figure was nearly as high, at 53,353, when car output would have been very limited and then varied in the range of around 38,000 to 47,000 for most of the war, high in the sense that these were trucks only.

The 1945 figure was down a little at 32,471 as military contracts eased off when the end of the war, at least in Europe, could be foreseen and peacetime orders, still at first subject to Government control, got under way, rising to 53,586 in 1946 and virtually equalling the 1939 figure at 61,453 in 1947. Then the 1948 figure was 74,576 and in 1949 it rose to 84,168, of which almost 39,000 were Bedfords. In 1950, a total of 40,429 Bedfords was reached, contributing to total Vauxhall and Bedford sales of 87,454. Some 63% of the Bedford output that year was for export – examples of the make were going to every continent, Africa becoming one of the most important markets. Some 12,693 post-war OB models were built up to November 1950, when production ceased, of which 5,493 were exported.

This was a remarkable performance, even though it was to be exceeded in later years, as Bedford's range widened even further, as will be explained in the next volume which brings the story up-to-date.

# Index

# Index

# Index

# Index

## VOLUME TWO

A second volume, to be published during 1996, will bring the Bedford story up-to-date. Starting in 1950 it will cover the SB range of buses, later bus developments, military and commercial vehicles, and the acquisition by AWD and, later, Marshalls. A comprehensive colour section will also be included, taking advantage of specialist material which came in to our possession during August 1995.

Reserve your copy now to avoid disappointment.

Venture Publications Ltd
128, Pikes Lane, Glossop, Derbyshire, SK13 8EH